R.E.F.R.E.S.H.I.N.G.

Change process

SLIM LAMBERT

ISBN: 1-4392-6911-4
ISBN-13: 9781439269114

TABLE OF CONTENTS

Thank you to friends and family for supporting me in the writing process.

1. PREAMBLE Q&A ABOUT THE 'R.E.F.R.E.S.H.I.N.G. CHANGE MANAGEMENT PROCESS' METHODOLOGY

1.1. Q. IN A NUTSHELL, WHAT IS THE REFRESHING CHANGE MANAGEMENT PROCESS?

REFRESHING stands for:

- Resistance free
- Empowering
- Fair
- Result focused
- Event based
- Solution focused
- High speed
- Involving
- Non-disruptive of delivery
- Guided by the people

These elements are the characteristics of the change management process proposed in this book.

It aims to be a process that is fast, fair, empowering and collaborative.

It is a way to address the fact that the current 80 % failure rate of change management processes, is not acceptable anymore because change management has become too important.

It is a new, radically different way of designing and driving a change management process. It could be summarised by one of the following principles:

- Leading change is not a heroic act.
- Forget top-down or directive leadership of the change process.
- Forget bottom-up or uncoordinated leadership of the change process.
- Do not use "pilots" to demonstrate feasibility or need for a change.
- People expect collaboration, transparency, and to have their voice heard—especially during change.
- *You* cannot change an organisation. People can change it, *with* you, if you honestly and fairly collaborate with them.
- *You* do not drive or define the change, *they* do.
- Change is always local, while you facilitate and drive it globally.
- Change management is between adults, not kids.
- Pull commitment; don't avoid resistance.
- Self-discovery, not "burning platforms," enables change.
- Forget the problem-focused change management processes.
- You don't want buy-in—that's just delaying the catastrophe and the relapse; you want commitment.
- *You* create resistance through the change *process* you use.

- Change management is more than two kilos of training and four kilos of communication; it is about tons of empowerment, fairness, involvement, and especially about meetings.
- Fairness of the change management process is not a "nice to have," it is a necessity.
- To hasten the change process, do things that you thought would slow it down.
- If it's not their change, they will not implement it, even if they initially wanted the change.
- Don't try to break resistance. Instead, let them create the energy of involvement.
- Don't sell the change to those who will need to change; let them sell it to you.
- Change is about framing differently what already works.
- Change is not about the quality of the solutions you propose, but about the questions you make those who will need to change ask themselves.
- Let them do the change, and give them the permission to do it.
- Change management that uses the wisdom of the crowds is implemented faster.
- Use "special" meetings efficiently, and change management becomes easy.
- If you give them the ownership and control, *you* will control and lead the change more.
- Change management is about action, not about talking, explaining, benchmarks, threats, and speeches—nobody believes them anymore, or for long.

- Nobody changes just because it's the right or reasonable thing to do.
- Change leaders are followers that lead through facilitation.
- Change is not painful, long, blocked by resistance, and so forth, unless you make it become that way.
- Change management need to follow to the Taoist sage Lao-tzu's principle: learn from the people, plan with them, begin with what they have, build on what they know.

1.1.1.   Q. What are the steps of the REFRESHING change management process and the tools used?

R.E.F.R.E.S.H.I.N.G stands for the characteristics and outputs of a change management process done in five steps and using some "special" meeting tools.

To make the change management process R.E.F.R.E.S.H.I.N.G, the five steps are:

1. Small-scale solutions and versions of the change
2. Vision of the change
3. Letting go of the old and doing new everyday actions
4. Sponsored projects
5. Burning bridges thanks to processes and culture

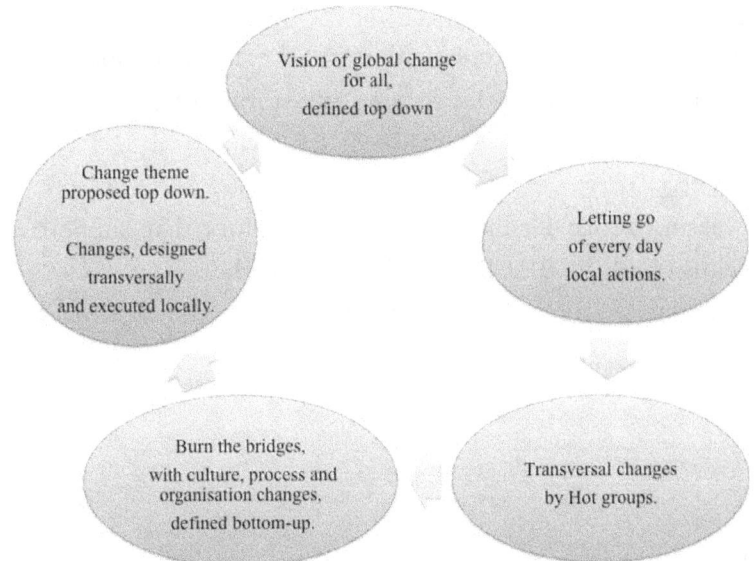

The corresponding meeting tools that will be used and the key acts are:

For step 1
Meeting tool: Implementable solutions to common future.

For step 2
Meeting tool: Define a draft of the vision of the applicable-to-all change.
Other acts: the leaders role model action plans.

For step 3
Meeting tools: work unit based dialogue workshops such as knowledge of the change café, open space meeting, or key behaviour workshop.

Slim Lambert

<u>For step 4</u>

Acts and meeting tools: pilots in the form of hot groups, followed by after actions reviews and storytelling.

<u>For step 5</u>

Meeting tools: Define a draft of the values that support the change and the Best Place to Work workshop.

Other acts: align processes and structure as an output to these meetings.

1.1.2. Q. What is change management?

It is a process aimed at planning, implementing, controlling, and stabilising changes in ways of doing work, processes, organisations, mindsets, or behaviours. It drives people's individual change process and commitment to the new solution embedded by the change. Solutions embedded in the change are largely uncertain at the beginning of the change process and emerge as products of the change effort itself.

The deliverables of the change management process are: the awareness of the need for change, the desire for change, the knowledge of what to do to change, the ability to change, and the belief that the change is reinforced by one's environment. These deliverables *are not steps* of the REFRESHING change management process. They are so interlinked that they cannot be distinguished in steps. However, each step of the REFRESHING change process enables organisations to reach these deliverables to different extents and on different scopes (local or global).

Q. If I use the REFRESHING change process, what will it change in the way I manage change?

The methodology directly challenges basic and often unstated assumptions that govern most current approaches. The latter have sadly become classic and accepted by most of us. The core tool of the REFRESHING change management process is "special" meeting tools, which enable people across the entire organisations to collaborate in crafting their collective change.

Research shows classic change management processes end up with a failure rate of 70 to 80 percent. This is the *failure* rate, not the success rate! The excuse given to explain this rate, is that change is complex or hard. I do not believe this sort of failure rates are accepted on any other topic in the business world. The current ways of managing change wastes energy and money, causes budget overruns, and results in disgruntled customers, demoralized employees, and stress for all. Things are probably even worse than the figures shown by various studies, as these studies rarely get the honest view of those who are expected to implement the change on a day-to-day basis. This also says a lot about how change is managed today!

Classic approaches to change do not work. Anything would be better. The main reason is the methodology used, that is, the process of doing change management. The classic change management approach talks about empowerment, making those that need to change see the change as a friend, change being an opportunity for growth and improvement, and as something that serves their interest. But the harsh reality is that it does not enable you to walk the talk, because of the underlying assumptions and tools used.

The REFRESHING process has proven to work and work very well. It turns the way we are used to managing change upside down. We should not focus on what leaders of a change want, but on what the people who will implement the change need. We need to empower and involve them. We need to avoid change that is dictated down to those who will implement it. Leaders should not design the change, but they should frame its design. All this is needed, not because we are naïve or nice people; it is just a pragmatic good business practice.

I believe leadership is the essence of successful change. But not the heroic or classic leadership to which we have become accustomed. Nowadays, change is an integral part of business life—of the way businesses functions. Change management cannot be disruptive to regular business nor can it be an additional project added to the organisation that delivers for the customer. We just do not have the luxury of considering change management that way. The change process needs to ensure fluidity and integration into people's everyday regular activities of delivering products and services. Sure, businesses are designed to work, not to change. But changing ways of working is an integral and recurrent part of this work.

Not every change is organisation-wide. Change can occur in a business unit, plant, group, or any segment of the organisation. So when I refer to the "organisation," it means whatever is within the boundary of the system that is undergoing the transformation. Any of these segments of the whole organisation is a system in and of itself, and even more importantly a part of a global system. This is underestimated, or not seen as a non-negotiable success factor in the classic way of managing change. Change, even in these smaller systems, must take into account the whole system.

Finally, classic organisational change is sometimes characterised as either *top-down* or *bottom-up*. The REFRESHING change management methodology isn't really either of these. Instead, it could be characterised as *middle-out*: everyone is involved and there is no preferred starting place. I do not believe that organisations can be changed according to plan or desire. The best we can do is to frame a direction or a focus point then build new connections and relationships so that self-management of the change can take place. This is driven by the leaders, and they can exercise a great deal of control on the situation. I will detail this in the next paragraphs.

The REFRESHING change management process embeds these ways of looking at implementing change.

I've implemented organisational change as a consultant and as internal change manager in major corporations. This enabled me to witness and reflect on what works and what does not. I've been able to differentiate between fallacious fears and true assumptions.

Do I know it all? Of course not. Have I applied the classic change management methods that fail more than 70 percent of the time? Sure I have. I've made most mistakes that any change manager can make. However, I've also tried some apparently extravagant and unfeasible change management roadmaps and tools that mentors have taught me. These mentors were sometimes considered to be extravagant, naïve, or unrealistic by elitist change experts of the time.

All this leads me to define and apply the REFRESHING process and discover that it works. I admit that it is not easy to go against conventional truths established by those who have a 70 or 80 percent failure rate! When you use the REFRESHING process, you will probably face hurdles and obstacles. But, let's face it, there are no simple solutions, and *the way we manage change today does not work.*

1.1.5. Q. Why read a book about change management?

Today, the ability to manage change is probably the number one barrier to progress and success factor for any organisation, big or small. We cannot stay put. We must change and adapt as our customers and markets change and as our competitors evolve. That is a truism if there ever was one!

1.1.6. *Q. What are the classic change management approaches you talk about?*

They come in different forms and variation. They use implicit principles such as "Tell people why they should change; if they do not comply, employ force or peer pressure to make them change. Pretend their opinion counts and symbolically indicate that it is in their best interest to comply." At the end of the day, those who need to change have little choice about the what, when, and how. Below are a couple of forms of classic change management approaches..

- **Top-down and directive.**

The leader or leadership team decides what the change is and how it will be implemented. They dramatically explain and communicate the change to those who will implement it. Sometimes, a selection of people—selected by the leaders!—are interviewed upfront or consulted to validate the pre-defined vision. So a collection of perceptions, those of the leaders and of those interviewed, is considered absolute truth on which the design and the implementation of the change will be based. The people interviewed are not given the opportunity to fine-tune their first opinions and ideas through constructive conflicts with peers and stakeholders. Nobody has the luxury the leaders have had—to digest both how to implement the change and the solution embedded in the change. But everybody is expected to understand and love the idea of changing, feel accountable, and feel committed to it. This of course jeopardizes the quality of the solutions embedded in the change that are dictated. They are often not feasible, too simplistic, or basically not the right thing to do. Nothing really happens, or people pretend that things change. They often take a stance of "We need extra resources; the solution provided to us is...," and so on. This frustrates leaders. They do not realise that it was they who created this dependency and procrastination by treating people like kids that cannot be trusted to make decisions for themselves or contribute with their information, point of view, or knowledge. People who ask questions are perceived as resisters. The leadership has or progressively builds a defensive "us against them" mindset. The extended leadership team and those interviewed could only make assumptions and inferences regarding the thoughts, needs, and ideas of those who will implement the change.

So what the change means for people's daily life is unclear for everyone, including the leaders. Change becomes something to avoid instead of something to embrace. It is perceived as a disruption to "real work." Change is an additional task and responsibility. Those responsible for managing it are perceived as detached from the true business issues. People who would need to change focus a lot of their time and energy on coping with how to react to the change being pushed down their throat. They focus less on the solution embedded in the change. Leaders complain about not being understood. They start thinking about firing people and bringing in new people. Poor communication about why and how to change is considered the key issues to address. But poor communication is only a consequence of the initial change process implemented by the change leaders.

- **Bottom-up and de-centralized.**

Teams of frontline workers are accountable and free to design and implement changes in the way they themselves work. There is no true framing of the issues in the interest of the whole organisation. Each of the parts of the organisation design the change as if they existed independently from the whole. It is every silo for itself! The implementation of these changes is done in a mode of "everyone for himself or herself." The gains are often at the expense of other parts of the organisation and sometimes the end customer. Sure, the "whole organisation" and the "end customer" are often used as excuses or distant indirect beneficiaries. But the neither are involved or consulted about the *what* and *how* of the change management! Changes are, therefore, not truly sustainable, and are seen as fads or ways for the leader to leave a legacy. People's commitment is to their silo-based changes because it is their change—they contributed to its design, planning, and implementation. In addition, they are in an "us against them" mindset toward colleagues in other parts of the organisation, who drive other change efforts too. Silos are reinforced. Each change in one part of the organisation seems trivial in scope or even nonexistent to others in the organisation and to those with a view of the whole organisation. The momentum and sustaining of local changes becomes an aspiration rather than a catalyst. The changes are

Slim Lambert

not fully implemented or sustained thanks to the alignment of global policies and culture. After a while, people's initial commitment dissipates because we human beings need to believe in or see an overall purpose if we are to be happy and committed to changing our individual behaviours. We need to understand the role of our actions in the unfolding drama of the whole organisation's fortunes and believe that it is worthwhile for us to play a part.

- **Cross-silo: another way of doing the top-down approach.**

Representatives of the silos of the organisation that will ultimately be affected by the top-down proposed change are recruited to help decide the what and how of the change. In the worst scenario, this is done after having tried a top-down approach. In the best scenario, it is done at the design step of the change before adopting a top-down approach. This collection of people is often supported and driven by consultants and is often called a task force, working group, diagonal slice group, subcommittee, or parallel organisation, or another similar name. What is created is another version of the top-down approach— the extended leadership team is replaced by people they have selected and who think like them.

- **Pilot-based: another way of doing a bottom-up approach.**

A specific part of the organisation is identified by the leaders, or is asked to volunteer, as the flagship or leader for change. Called "pilots," these change efforts benefit from having a well-defined task, the attention and support of organisation leaders, and the allocation of resources required to ensure success. This is another version of the bottom-up change, to which is added the drawbacks of the top-down approach. Pilots prove difficult to transfer to other parts of the organisation. In addition, the impact on the whole organisation is not the one imagined by just extrapolating from a pilot. The latter is linked to the way "complex systems" work. You cannot analyse, manage, or change a system based on a few of its isolated components. At least three principles are ignored when you do not apply the latter. First, even if all components adopt a behaviour or way of working, this does not result in the same collective behaviour or ways of working for the system. Second, a change in one component of a system has unintended and unexpected consequences for the whole system and its other components. Third, one component's success or change is dependent on how it interacts with the strengths and weaknesses of its environment, so, if you ask the environment to change the initial success of change is jeopardized.

Q. I'VE ALWAYS THOUGHT THAT CHANGE MANAGEMENT IS ALL ABOUT MANAGING RESISTANCE TO CHANGE. HOW CAN THE **REFRESHING** CHANGE PROCESS MAKE THE PROCESS RESISTANCE FREE?

First, lets recall the steps of the REFRESHING change management process:
(1) Small-scale solutions and versions of the change; (2) vision of the change; (3) letting go of the old and doing new everyday actions; (4) sponsored projects; and (5) burning bridges thanks to processes and culture

Resistance management is a self-fulfilling prophecy and a myth. It is *you* who manages a change that is creating it through the *process you use. Resistance is avoidable!* The objective of managing change should be to build commitment, not reduce or mitigate the effects of resistance.

Commitment is agreeing or pledging to do something in the future, and feeling obligated or emotionally impelled to stick with it. It includes having ownership and power to perform "my" corresponding local daily tasks while collectively sharing a common ground or a higher purpose with others.

You can actually create commitment. *You* can never truly "kill" resistance once you have created it. Once resistance is there, it becomes part of the identity and social role of those who resist. It is a very strong role, because it creates a lot of positive and negative "strokes" as they say in the "transactional analysis" methodology.

But more importantly, change requires people to go beyond their habitual ways of doing. It also requires creativity and solution finding. Lack of major resistance is just not enough to make people do this. So even if you control them every minute of the day, they won't really implement a change if they are not committed it. They can pretend. At best, they will play it safe and do the minimal things to avoid being labelled as resistant.

If there is no commitment, people relapse to the old ways when faced with difficulties, uncertainties, or (slight) stress. Buy-in or lack of resistance does not stand the test of facing stress, uncertainty, hesitancy, pressure, behavioural change, dilemma management, self-interest over the collective interest, action that needs resilience or even just effort, and so on. All these things are part of business as usual, and they are even more intense and frequent if change is needed!

Do people change what or who they are? You could argue that they do not. I don't know. What is certain is that they adapt to their environment, and every organisation is an environment. With the possible exception of the cockroach, humans are the most adaptable species on the planet. Humans by their very nature must try to figure out what the new environment demands and work out some solution to make it happen. They do not resist this if you use the right process because you use as lever their natural survival instinct.

So "how to manage resistance" is the wrong question to ask! People resist change in the classic ways of managing change, but they don't really resist changing. They resist change being imposed on them, and they resent being tricked into being falsely empowered, or if they perceive the change process as unfair. The real enemy of change management is *apathy*, not resistance to change. The attitude of "Just tell me what you want done, boss, so I can get out of this place and on with my real life" is what kills organisational life and, even more, the implementation of a change. The REFRESHING change management process gives them the choice to remain or not in apathy. Few do not jump on the opportunity to control their lives if you let them chose the way to do it within a frame proposed by the leader who proposes a "theme" to address. I detail this concept of "theme" later in the book.

Some people like stability. But they know through their everyday experience that stability requires changing to recreate it. The REFRESHING change management process pulls them into translating this awareness into acts of change within their local and daily scope.

Everyone needs to grow, to be stimulated, to find solutions, to create a better future, and to be useful for others. These things are provided through the REFRESHING change management process.

If you believe that people thrive on change, you will tap into a limitless source of ingenuity, energy, and a solution-focused mindset. When managing change, you need to aim for building commitment to the change. You first encourage commitment to local daily acts, to seeing things differently, to innovating, and to looking for solutions. As a result, people become committed to the change you imagined was needed. You want a change management process that enables everyone to make decisions about finding day-to-day solutions they can implement in order to contribute to a theme proposed by the organisation and its leaders.

Commitment ensures that people act in an autonomous and accountable way to serve their interests and those of the organization. Autonomy does not mean independent, selfish, or win-lose actions. Commitment renders people willing to put forth extraordinary amounts of time and energy to reach a common goal. Committed people make things happen. Commitment is a product of the REFRESHING change management process. *It is created at step 1 of the REFRESHING change management process and is nurtured during the next steps of the process.*

1.2.1   *Q. I've always thought that it was necessary to create a crisis or a burning platform for people to let go of resistance and buy in to a change. Isn't this the case?*

No, that's a myth. Again, what you should aim for is commitment, not lack of resistance. *Fear never creates sustainable commitment.* It might create a smoke screen of short-lived buy in or alignment. Crisis and fear triggers running away, paralysis, or attack. None of these emotions or acts create commitment. When afraid, people do not focus on how to contribute to the change; they waste time and energy focusing on how to react to the one who brings fear on them. They do not focus on what really matters: designing and implementing the new solutions embedded in the change. Moreover, elements such as crisis and fear are, by definition, limited in time and amount. And as time passes, people get used to them or find ways to live with or bypass them. They return to the old habits and patterns.

Commitment requires something completely different in nature. For example, in my career as a physician, I witnessed that the desire to feel good and live a full life drives sustainable change. It is not the fear in the first few weeks after a heart attack or a cancer scare that breeds a change in patients' lifestyles. They must find a higher purpose.

At best, a crisis provides the context or the argument for leaders to convince themselves and their stakeholders about their idea of a change needs to be considered. But this is not enough to make the idea of change a reality. They need to become aware of which habits, often virtually unconscious to them, are no longer appropriate to the organisation's changed circumstances. They need to become convinced that they can implement new ways and that doing so is better than the status quo. This requires a true change management process, and not just informing the organisation about a crisis or a new "fadish" solution, which the organisation will resist, and rightfully so. So would you in their shoes.

With the REFRESHING change management process, people become committed and have the desire to implement a new state in a way that you probably never expected if you've just used the burning platform or a crisis as lever.

You cannot tell people to change. We all know that. *We need to walk the talk* and enable people to think by themselves, understand the idea behind the need to change, and experiment with the change on the business-as-usual topics *they* have chosen. In a nutshell, the leaders should not create a sense of urgency. They need to create commitment among people and then let them design and implement the change. This generates a sense of urgency in the people that is much stronger than any generated by fear or threats.

How do you create this commitment? One of the key levers to creating commitment is the opportunity to be involved in a true dialogue. *Dialogue* is enabled in each step of the REFRESHING change management process.

1.2.2.   *Q. How can dialogue build commitment?*

Used in the context of the REFRESHING change management process, dialogue enables people to talk about concrete, everyday elements of change that are important to them. And when we say talk about, I do not mean debate or argue, which are ways of talking are no more than unproductive power games.

Dialogue is a way of escalating each person's cognitive conflict through challenge and critique of his or her approach toward business and task-related issues while de-escalating affective conflict. Dialogue enables common goals, values, and norms to surface. It makes people feel they are working together on things that serve each one's interests. Dialogue should always take place in groups of a size that allows for manageable discussion about task-related change topics. It will never be generated without provoking conflict escalation. The notion of provoking conflict escalation turns the traditional view of "resistance" on its head. Without some level of conflict, the management of the change will, at best, under-deliver on your expectations or, at worst, bring you only to cynicism and helplessness. Dialogue is not about smooth interaction or the suppression of conflict. Nor is it about "soliciting ideas and feedback" while not letting those who gave the ideas act on them. It is this airing of differences, divergent opinions, good ideas, criticisms, and the like that create commitment, if done the right way. Meeting tools proposed in the REFRESHING process all enable true dialogue, thanks to their structure and animation flow.

During these meeting tools, a lot of things happen that create and sustain commitment thanks to true dialogue. To mention just a few:

- People work with people they know, respect, or admire.
- People have an active role inside the framework of the meeting. They influence the content strongly. They set or adjust the agenda or the topics addressed. So the outputs are consistent with their own set of values.
- Facts are discovered and given meaning during the meetings, not thrown in people's faces.
- People connect and interact during the meetings in ways that create the desire to bond and act together after the meeting.

- People select and identify, by themselves, the change actions they will implement after the meeting—in agreement with and with the full commitment of the representatives of the "whole" organisation.
- People become convinced that the change actions they implement contribute to changes that will occur and have an impact.

This is key, because people do not want to waste their time and effort, or be part of a process with unclear objectives. And they don't want to be part of something for which their personal contribution is minor.

- People will see positive results from their efforts during the meeting.
- People will identify actions based on the analysis of actions they and the whole organisation took in the past. They will learn and feel that the needed change is not a blaming game..
- People will benefit from social support provided by peers and stakeholders who work with them to come up with the proposal of changes.
- People will be empowered to create a compelling purpose for change that is crystal clear, because it has been discussed and thought through in depth and in concrete terms related to how it could be implemented.
- Commitment to building the future will be created by honouring the past and present.
- Commitment will be created by building relationships across existing silos and hierarchical levels.

Slim Lambert

- People will see concrete opportunities that show that their voice counts on topics that are important for them.
- People will discover the "whole" organisation's interests, concerns, and opinions.
- People will be part of a constructive conflict escalation that creates trust and insight.
- People will express their emotions, positive and negative, inherent to learning.

These emotions are prompted through the sequencing of activities of the meeting tools: when people build insight about the issues that are affecting them, they experience both depression and excitement. They become depressed about the complexity of the issues facing them, wondering how they will ever deal effectively with them; then they become excited about the possibilities for doing things differently. People will have time for interaction and dialogue so that they can absorb the meaning of new information or information that proves the need for a change. People will learn and discover together, and begin to feel smart about the issues facing them. When people feel smart, they act smartly, take control of situations and problems, and develop creative solutions.

1.2.3.   *Q. What characterises the discussions that take place in the meeting tools used in the REFRESHING change management process?*

It is a discussion that:

- provides an environment that is familiar (meetings are probably the things you do most in an organisation);

- provides an agenda that seems classic and common-sense based, while the exercises and activities inside the agenda are chosen in a specific manner;
- focuses on questions that matter to participants, not just to the host;
- iterates between advocacy and inquiry;
- is focused on the business objective and strategy, while working on what it means at the level of each participant;
- does not threaten people's careers;
- is structured to ensure high creativity inside the frame defined by the structure of the meeting;
- pulls participants to really listen to each other's viewpoints and not get into polarizing arguments;
- ensures that each participant is confronted with many different perspectives, and thus, has enough information to make good decisions for the whole and for themselves.
- creates the glue, energy, and confidence for communities of action to be launched after the meeting;
- guides participants into discovering the need for change by realizing that they actually might know how to solve problems in a new context;
- pulls participants into discovering solutions that already work in the new context;
- gives the opportunity for participants to share with others the "if-onlys," "why-nots," and "what-is" considered "impossible" before the meeting;
- reveals the often puzzling patterns of incoherence that lead a group or a participant to avoid certain issues or, on

the other hand, to insist, against all reason, on standing and defending opinions about particular issues;

- gives an opportunity for participants to observe collectively how hidden values and intentions can control their behaviour and how unnoticed beliefs and assumptions can clash without them realizing it;
- slows down the process of participants' thought in order for them to be able to observe it while it is actually occurring (Different cognitive biases can surface. For example, they witness the halo effect, risk aversion, placebo effect, self-fulfilling prophecy, and many others.);
- creates a sense of increased harmony, fellowship, and "being in this together";
- ensures collaboration and the intellectual and emotional involvement of all participants, that it's not about a theory or an idea, but about the planning of actions and the committing to them;
- ensures that decisions are taken by participants with a systemic understanding of the context and backgrounds;
- builds the willingness of participants to explore and gain a deep insight into a situation or theme;
- ensures that participants search for solutions, not problems;
- makes it impossible for hierarchical leaders to give monologue-like speeches or to take the control of what happens during the discussions;
- gives any participant the possibility to take leadership in implementing agreed actions after the meeting;

- encourages participants to avoid considering the way they interpret the world as the only sensible way it can be interpreted, even if the context has changed;
- helps participants express their reactions and feelings about the needed organisational change and how to address this need;
- frees the flow of information and the expression of feelings about the proposed theme and the participants' context;
- first enhances participants' anxiety about the current situation, the provides immediate opportunity, thanks to other participants, for relief by engaging in concrete actions of change;
- enables participants to see their contribution to organisational problems and solutions;
- creates "permeability" in the organisation by encouraging communication and information flow across formal hierarchies and functions represented by participants of the meeting;
- suspends, for a while, participants' judgments (It does not mean repressing, suppressing or even postponing them—it means giving them serious attention so that their structures can be noticed.);
- ensures that the conversations are among equals (Organisational leaders, stakeholders, customers, providers, doers, coordinators, etc. are participants just like everybody else.);
- forces all participants to talk about the same world as they discover others' perspectives, as the others present

the whole system relevant for the theme addressed, and as participants back up their opinions with examples;

- guides participants to discover common needs, desires, and implementable actions.

1.2.4.   *Q. Do you aim for consensus through dialogue during the meetings about methodology?*

No. *You aim for informed decision-making. And dialogue provides the vehicle to discover common ground.* There may be things that people disagree on, but they also learn that there is a wide space of agreement within which they are able to take a coordinated set of actions.

Dialogue differs from debate in that the goal is not to define whose ideas are right or to create homogeneity of opinions. Rather it is to encourage the emergence of a diversity of ideas, which cultivates innovation and creativity. The goal is understanding and then acting. It empowers and involves everyone affected by the decisions taken. The result is higher quality decision making, more support, better flexibility, and openness to new ideas. The process of holding multiple perspectives open for discussion creates tension within the group, which drives group members to strive for understanding. Working toward a shared understanding expands an individual's tolerance for opinions different from his or her own. Dialogue equalises power differentials among people and shuns expert opinion. Participants express uncertainties as well as deeply held beliefs. Participants listen to understand and gain insight into the beliefs and concerns of the others. Questions are asked from a position of curiosity.

1.2.5. *Q. Are their scales of commitment? Is there strong and weak commitment? If so, what does the methodology do about it?*

Yes, commitment can vary in depth. You want to build a *deep and lasting commitment* to the change. In the context of change management, it is characterised by:

- a thorough understanding of the logic and reasons for local translations of the change needed at the organisational level;
- an alignment of the change with own personal beliefs, values, and motivations;
- a personal attachment to the person doing the persuading (In the REFRESHING change management process, that person is not the leader, but the people themselves or other peers.);
- a desire to learn how to implement the new solution embedded in the change;
- trust in one's ability to implement the change;
- a solution-focused approach to the issues the change addresses, instead of problem-focused framing of these issues;
- little questioning or doubt about what needs to be done on a day-to-day basis to live and breathe the change;
- resilience in adopting the new ways of doing things'
- desire for concrete actions to implement the change;

- desire to embark others on the search for solutions that will stretch one's comfort zone as one changes or discovers how to change;
- belief that something new is better than something that one masters or is comfortable with.

Attaining deep commitment usually has a cost. It requires smart investment of time and energy—paradoxically, not a huge amount of it. The meeting tools are a way to invest that time.

First, lets recall the steps of the REFRESHING change management process:
(1) Small-scale solutions and versions of the change; (2) vision of the change; (3) letting go of the old and doing new everyday actions; (4) sponsored projects; (5) burning bridges thanks to processes and culture.

The risk lies in not empowering! The key to successful change management and commitment is not that you explain things to people. It is that they discover things by themselves. The safest thing, and the one that yields the highest return on investment, is to first *define a theme that requires change. Then, to let those who will need to change contribute to define and implement the what and how of the needed change, to decide if the change is realistic, and to decide how to best live with this change.* Machiavelli (1469-1527) said, "There is nothing more difficult to take in hand, more perilous to conduct, or more uncertain in its success, than to take the lead in the introduction of a new order of things, because the innovator has for enemies all those who have done well under the old conditions, and lukewarm defenders in those who may do well under the new." So none of us should bang our heads on the wall and try to push a change down the throat of people. The change management process needs to pull them into being committed to a change. The PROCESS therefore needs to be transparent, respectful, and fair. This will create the conditions for people to take the opportunity to be empowered to come up with the new solutions embedded in the change. The REFRESHING change process enables them to do this.

1.3.1. Q. So the goal of empowering is to create accountability?

Yes, but it is not the only goal. And *it is more a benefit created by the fact that people are committed.* The complexity of change and the difficulty of controlling it must be countered by making all those who will implement it accountable for it. No single person or group of people can maintain control or anticipate every development of the change process, nor can they make all the right decisions during the process. So it is imperative that you have confidence in those involved and trust their abilities. This is the seed for their desire to become accountable.

1.3.2. Q. What are people empowered to do?

Too often, small numbers of people—and often the wrong ones—closet themselves in secrecy, hatch grand schemes, and then unleash them on an unprepared and uncooperative organisation. Too often, executives rush to seize on a particular set of strategic choices of the change without generating full discussion of all the possible alternatives. Too many organisations make crucial decisions about change based on incomplete and biased information. The design and implementation of a change is hard work by all, not just by a few.

The REFRESHING change management process therefore creates the conditions for people to be empowered to *first decide about the design and the implementation of what a change means locally for them, and to ensure its speed.* Based on the reality test of the latter, they are then empowered to contribute to *design and define the change needed for the whole organisation* (what I call the applicable-to-all change). Remember that no change can be considered outside of the "whole" of which it is a part.

This does not mean that all opinions will prevail. It means that people's perceptions and needs will be taken into account and that those impacted by a decision will have the opportunity to influence it. Involvement occurs in ways that empower. Involvement in decision making is genuine. Everyone has the opportunity to express himself or herself and to be heard. Full involvement enables people to understand the objectives of a change and to express their reservations, fears, and opposition. It also enables them to feel that they have the power to influence their own future and to strengthen their sense of belonging to a group.

1.3.3. *Q. Does empowering people through the REFRESHING change management process create what is called "intrinsic motivation" and/ or the belief in the benefits or feasibility of the change?*

Yes. *Empowerment creates commitment and commitment creates intrinsic motivation; and intrinsic motivation creates beliefs.* People need to believe in the new solutions or ways of doing. Getting people to change is getting them to make a bet on the future and, therefore, believe that the unknown will be better for them.

With extrinsic motivation, people go along for reasons other than belief in a future, for example, because of associated rewards and punishments. In theory, extrinsic motivation creates behavioural changes, which create a mindset change after enough time. One advantage with extrinsic motivation is that it can be generated relatively quickly and on demand. However, it has its strong limitations. It generates compliance, not commitment, and often, defensive reactions, and people do not change in a sustainable manner. They put in just enough effort—mostly visible and simplistic—to secure the rewards they seek and avoid the punishments they fear. Extrinsic motivation dissipates once the external levers are removed. Therefore *the change of mindset rarely has the time to occur despite the theoretical assumptions about extrinsic motivation.*

In the REFRESHING change process, extrinsic motivation levers are used, but they are not used as key levers. They are used as ad-hoc accelerating tactics limited in time and scope. Indeed, it is more efficient to *take the time to build intrinsic motivation and then afterwards, use extrinsic levers to reinforce or accelerate the building of commitment to a change.*

Intrinsic motivation drives sustainable mindset change, which leads to behaviour change. This is even more true if the "whole" adopts acts or beliefs that are coherent with the change.

Failure to create intrinsic motivation is the usual pitfall of classic change management approaches. Intrinsic motivation occurs when people are genuinely convinced of the need for change and the benefits of doing so. It does not rely on the monetary incentives used to create extrinsic motivation. It occurs when people have the opportunity to unleash energy, enthusiasm, and creativity. It requires that people discover and identify the proof by themselves of reasons for the change.

For example, during the meetings tool, people discover that peers and stakeholders believe the change is feasible and worth it. They also discover the unseen promises of reward and risks of status quo. After the meeting tools, they practice the actions of change defined by these beliefs. This, added to the discoveries made, creates and sustains people's belief in the change.

Beliefs cannot be dictated. So, the REFRESHING change management process creates the conditions that facilitate or accelerate the creation of these beliefs amongst the people who need to implement a change. Three levels of beliefs are created. Level one is the belief in the need for organisational change. Level two is the belief in the feasibility of this change. And level three is the belief in the need for personal change in order to contribute to this change.

1.3.4.   *Q. I've tried participative management but it does not work. Do you really think people will rise up to being empowered?*

It is the sequence or the steps and the tools used in the REFRESHING change management process that make people rise up to the challenge. They reciprocate being empowered. It is not the charisma or smarts of a leader or change manager.

It is true that today, people hesitate to "rise up" to being empowered. They have been taught by their environment that they cannot or should not truly be empowered. This is taught at early stages of life, for example in the way the schools teach and select what to teach. Then in corporate and social life, the excuse used to not empowering people is that some cannot be trusted, that some authority knows best, that they will not be able or want to understand the whole picture. To overcome this misconception, people need a democratic-like and empowering environment in which to learn how to act when truly empowered. People learn how to act in an empowered way by being truly allowed to be empowered. The REFRESHING change management process provides the environment that, for example, kills one key misconception, which is that an elite group of experts or leaders know what people who will implement a change should do and how to do it. This environment is one that uses democratic-like principles in a pragmatic and realistic manner that suits the business organisational world.

When one claims that people might not be ready to get involved and become empowered, it is more the result of a self-fulfilling prophecy than a hard fact. People who have not been fully and genuinely empowered in the past will hesitate to rise to the opportunity. And remember, the organisation benefits as much if not more than the people themselves when people rise up to being empowered!

In the past, when organisations enticed people to get involved in "participative management" efforts, *they did not provide the conditions for democratic-like authority structures.* The term itself suggests that there is no empowerment expected. Instead, you subtly manipulate, co-opt, persuade, or even coerce people to accept a plan or decision that was already made by elitist experts. Participative management was devised primarily as a technique of persuasion to accept decisions that had already been made by management. It enables organisations to get a clarification of people's understanding and, thus, improve the way management can get their obedience. These schemes amount to subtle forms of coercion and manipulation. And people know pretended empowerment when they see it!

It is okay that the final decision or the arbitration is made by leaders. What is not okay is that people are not empowered to act on decisions they have contributed to take. What is not okay and that these actions do not influence the final decision that will be taken by leadership.

If denied the opportunity to be responsible for their own behaviour, people will behave irresponsibly. This is a rational response! However, when the same people find themselves in a context where they can take responsibility for their behaviour, they typically do so. The REFRESHING change management process creates a democratic-like environment that empowers. People have equal rights to determine ends and purposes and to make decisions regarding the means to achieve them. They all have a voice, the power, and the real possibility to influence the final say with regard to setting priorities, making decisions, and formulating action plans that impact them.

Q. Do leaders lose control if they empower people? Does the organisation have to take recommendations into account? What is the degree of authority of leaders?

Leaders are free to decide how much of their power and control they want to share with the people who will need to implement a change. That is not an issue if it is stated up-front, in order to avoid to discredit the act of asking people to become committed to the change. The **REFRESHING** change management process is flexible with regard to how much decision making power leaders share, but it needs to be stated up-front.

What remains constant, however, is that if leaders do not accept an idea, they have to say why. People need to feel that their voice has been heard and their views have been taken seriously and incorporated in the what and how of the change. *If that is not the case, do not waste their and the organisation's time try to build commitment to a change.*

"Loss of control" actually rarely becomes an issue because leaders quickly discover that they control the situation thanks to the frame defined by the theme on which people get involved. In the **REFRESHING** process, all starts with the fact that people work on a theme and discover if and what change is needed inside that theme. At the end of the day, leaders have more control of the change process than when they direct it using classic change management approaches!

Will people not start wondering, "Is anybody in charge here? Doesn't somebody have some idea where this place is going?" No, because the global *what* is clear, that is, the theme and "how to get there." People then are empowered to define this locally and to influence the fine-tuning of the theme. What is open for participation is how to get there. *This satisfies people's need to be active participants in shaping their future while craving for strong leadership.* Maybe someday that will change, but today, considerable research indicates that the most effective leaders are those who are absolutely clear, direct, and non-participatory in the what (labelled for example as direction, priorities, or vision) yet tremendously open about how the group (or the organisation) gets there through the daily acts and behaviours of its people.

In the REFRESHING change management process, leaders do not stand up and tell people, "I don't have a clear vision. I don't know where we're going. Let's work together and develop a vision by committee." That would lead only to fear, uncertainty, stress, anxiety, and a loss of confidence in the leadership.

Instead, they say to their people, "Let me tell you what my vision is. Let me tell you what kind of company I want to build. Let me explain to you how I reached that conclusion. This implies we need to work on a couple of themes. Now I want to work with all of you on figuring out how we get there. To address some of these themes we will work together according to a process called the REFRESHING management process. The first step is discovering together what need to be done about the theme X."

Q. Do you go as far as to empower people to design of the vision of the needed change?

Yes. In today's complex environment, *it is probably not realistic to expect that one person can create an effective vision for an entire organisation.* What is needed is to involve at least a critical mass of people who have different roles at many levels of the organisation, as well as stakeholders and customers. In addition, a great vision is of no use if it is not implementable or implemented. So, before deciding to implement a vision, its feasibility and the resources required need to be assessed in order to fine-tune the level of ambition of the vision. This assessment is best done by the people who will translate the vision into reality on a daily basis. It is best done if it is based on small-scale local attempts by these people to translate the vision into reality. Both of these things are achieved thanks to step 1 of the **REFRESHING** change management process. Step 1 gives people the autonomy to determine appropriate means for defining and implementing the vision of the needed change. *This vision is roughly defined through the theme proposed by the leader.*

A lot is learned from getting the opinions and input of people throughout the organisation. People have good ideas about how the organisation can be improved. After all, they "are" the organisation.

As the business world becomes more complex, the efforts of a single leader are likely to be less important than the coordinated efforts of the motivated employee base. The performance of any company depends on the strength of each of its component units, as well as on the effectiveness of their integration. This is also true for the design, not only for the implementation of a project or an idea. *Empowerment allows for a guided discovery of the vision.*

Q. ORGANISATIONAL LIFE IS NOT 'FAIR' OR DEMOCRATIC, SINCE IT'S ABOUT DELIVERING A RESULT AND MAKING PROFIT. SO HOW CAN THE **REFRESHING** PROCESS STAND FOR FAIRNESS?

First, lets recall the steps of the REFRESHING change management process:
(1) Small-scale solutions and versions of the change; (2) vision of the change; (3) letting go of the old and doing new everyday actions; (4) sponsored projects; and (5) burning bridges thanks to processes and culture

You are correct about organisational life. The fairness we are talking about is the fairness of the *process*, not necessarily the outcome.

Experience demonstrates that people will go against their own self-interest if they feel something violates the notions they have about fairness and justice of the process that produces the outcome. *The outcome is close to unimportant for people compared to the process to reach the outcome!*

Fairness of process means working together in a way that blurs the privileges associated with roles and titles. Everyone has an equal responsibility for contributing to the outcome. And when making decisions, everyone has an equal voice. It means everyone has an equal opportunity to participate in the change process to the degree they desire. It means you believe that experts and leaders have answers, but not the only answers, or necessarily the best ones, especially regarding the day-to-day issues of the organisation's people. Everyone is an expert at something—at a minimum, their daily work conditions and constraints.

In the mid-1970s, social scientists John W. Thibaut and Laurens Walker combined their research on the psychology of justice and the study of process to look at what makes people trust a legal system enough to follow its laws voluntarily. They discovered that people care as much about the fairness of the process as the outcome that process generates. However, they can live with and be committed to a tough outcome if the process to reach it is fair. But they will not be committed to a good outcome if the process to reach it is not fair.

Empowerment, as defined in the REFRESHING change management process, is key for a process to be perceived as fair. It is *the* tangible proof of three criteria that create the perception of fairness of a process: involvement, explanation, and expectation clarity.

Involvement. People want to be involved in the decisions that affect them. They want to provide input and be allowed to review decisions actively, ideally with peers. They want to be respected for their ideas.

Explanation. People want to understand the reasons for decisions that affect them and with which they are involved. They want to understand why their input has been considered, or why it is not. They want proof that final choices have been made impartially in the overall interest of the whole (the organisation, group, or end customer, for example). For people to be committed to these choices, they need to feel congruence. So they need to have an active role in deciding on the final choices. Explanation is not about just giving an explanation, but about helping people discover and build the explanation.

Expectation clarity. Once a decision is made, people want clarity about their responsibilities and their leaders' expectations.

1.4.1. *Q. Do you want to create a democracy?*

No. Of course, organisations are not democracies and leaders of the organisation are not elected representatives. Hierarchies with authority for decision-making are needed for organisations to be efficient. That's a no-brainer. Democracy is the best form we humans have developed for people to come together, discuss, resolve issues, and act. What we will use in the REFRESHING change management process are its underlying principles, adapted to the corporate world. These democratic-like principles produce trust and commitment in the change process and in those leading it.

With the REFRESHING change management process, you do not aim for consensus decision-making about local translations of the change or expect that the final decision about the applicable-to-all change will be put to a vote. The REFRESHING change management process does not intend or require that everyone vote on everything or that leaders act like elected officials. That would bring organisations to their knees.

Democratic-like principles ensure the free flow of information, avoid secret decision-making, allow people affected by a decision to influence it, and allow people to regroup and dialogue about issues important to them in order to make proposals and take action.

1.4.2.   Why is having a fair process important when you manage change?

First, a fair process builds commitment. People will go above and beyond the call of duty or volunteering, where before they would have to be coerced. This is key in times of change. It enables organisations to capitalise on people's talent, knowledge, and desire to design and implement a change.
People will forget what you said, people will forget what you did, but they will never forget how you made them feel. In other words, the need for a fair process corresponds to the need to feel important, heard, respected, and believe that one has not been treated as a resource.

Second, a fair process builds trust. Change requires trust; that is a no-brainer. The fairness of the change management process demonstrates that you trust people. So, you make the first "gift" of trust before people are asked to reciprocate and take the risk to trust you enough to embark on a change. Trust begets trust.

Q. Change management is too confusing and uncertain to be 'result focused,' don't you think?

First, lets recall the steps of the REFRESHING change management process:
(1) Small-scale solutions and versions of the change; (2) vision of the change; (3) letting go of the old and doing new everyday actions; (4) sponsored projects; and (5) burning bridges thanks to processes and culture.

Every step is about producing action plans or involving people in projects that deliver the solutions embedded in the change. The people drive the process, so there is no need for great speeches or other communication efforts. *The focus is on action and action only.*

There are meetings during which people talk and plan. As we will see, *discussion is action* and enables action and, therefore, results.

First, lets recall the steps of the REFRESHING change management process:
(1) Small-scale solutions and versions of the change; (2) vision of the change; (3) letting go of the old and doing new everyday actions; (4) sponsored projects; and (5) burning bridges thanks to processes and culture.

The main tools used in the REFRESHING process are meeting tools. They enable two things.

First, they enable an organisation to build commitment, self-managed discovery, true dialogue, trust, a sense of belonging, learning, a focus on solutions, a feeling of accountability, defining immediate actions after the insight that there is a need for change, empowerment, and the necessary process of individual transition. They enable this thanks to the structure of the meeting tools.

Second, they enable organisations to regroup a number of people that can range from ten to two-thousand at the same time. They enable involvement of a critical mass of the people affected by change, both inside the organisation (employees and management) and outside it (suppliers and customers).

No. The meeting tools used in the REFRESHING change management process are not like any regular meeting. Meetings are structured in specific ways to ensure dialogue as defined in the previous paragraphs. In these meetings, peer pressure and peer learning is nurtured and enhanced. People put their self-interest aside and work for the common good. No written statement or inspiring speech about the change is delivered. The dialogue produces understanding, excitement, engagement, and commitment to implementing change actions.

Connections made during these meetings are the oil that lubricates the wheels of organisational life during the design and implementation of the change. Spending time developing connections, especially during periods of change, is not a nice-to-have, it's a must-have investment!

The REFRESHING change management process uses a tool that is already part of people's regular work activities: *meetings. It just uses them differently.* A meeting is the thing that today's organisations use the most—but inefficiently.

The meetings tools used in the REFRESHING process are not like classic meetings. For example:

- The host plans the structure and processes of the meeting but lets the content take care of itself.
- People who attend the meeting are active participants, not an audience.

- Attendance is voluntary.
- As many participants as needed are involved to get the required variety of information and level of participant commitment. Meetings remain efficient with as many as two-thousand participants at one meeting.
- The participants—not the sponsor, the chairman or the speakers—are responsible for what is achieved in the meeting, its agenda, and the time spent on parts of the meeting.
- Risk-taking during a meeting is essential and deliberately prompted.
- Participants are helped to move through chaos and discover the creativity and learning that they possess. The goal is not to keep everything under control, minimize risks, or avoid chaos at all costs.
- Participants communicate among themselves, not with the speaker, sponsor, or chairman.
- Participants have come to pool their knowledge. So it's okay for facilitators to show their ignorance.
- Participants have not come to get answers that some experts will provide through a series of presentations.
- Participants are given enough time and opportunity to connect with each other, building a sense of community.
- Although there are times when it's appropriate to create sub-groups, the rule of thumb is that all participants are kept together.
- Participants all have access to the same information and have a shared experience of discovery and action planning.

The facilitators are responsible for the climate and the momentum. Actually, the structure of the meeting tools creates the climate and the momentum. *They ensure the respect of the flow and sequencing of the activities during the meeting.* So, yes, almost anybody can animate these meetings.

What are the different things to which a facilitator pays attention or can influence? Facilitators manage task assignments and large group dialogues and dynamics. Participants manage everything else. They are the ones to implement the actions afterward, so you want to do as little as possible and let them take responsibility for their own work from the start.

The facilitators ensure there is a climate of hospitable space. They can try anything that breaks away from the regular work environment and creates a comfortable hospitable space where people can move around inside. For example, place flowers on the tables, use red-checked tablecloths, small vases, palm trees and other greenery, make banners with different quotes on them, play music, and so on.

The facilitators hand out guidelines for the activities during the meeting. For example, they hand out the ground rules of the meeting while ensuring that they are read and discussed. Their role is not to read them out and explain them. It is to hand them out and make people talk about them in small groups before talking about them in the whole group. For example, they ask participants to take turns in reading the introduction sections aloud. Doing this prepares the group to participate and creates an environment that encourages participation. It also prepares participants for working in small groups and sharing for the whole group.

The ground rules are always the same:

- All perceptions are valid during the idea-generation phases.
- If you have an opinion and someone else has a contrary opinion, that's fine. Post them on a flipchart. You will have time to discuss these, and battle it out if necessary. You do not have to agree on everything. What you are aiming to accomplish is a common community product.
- Data generation has to be public and put on flipcharts or posters. Everything is discussed publicly; there is no room for hidden agendas.
- Listen to each other.
- Observe time frames.
- Seek common ground and action.
- Each small group manages its own discussion, data, time, and reports.

What the role of the facilitator is *not,* is, for example: telling people what is appropriate to bring up; reconciling disagreements; judging the relevance or usefulness of a statement; interpreting peoples' comments; acting as a process consultant on interpersonal dynamics; challenging peoples' motives or assumptions; or taking positions with respect to content.

First, lets recall the steps of the REFRESHING change management process:
(1) Small-scale solutions and versions of the change; (2) vision of the change; (3) letting go of the old and doing new everyday actions; (4) sponsored projects; and (5) burning bridges thanks to processes and culture.

During the meetings of the REFRESHING change management process, *a problem-solving mindset is avoided. Instead, the mindset that is created is one of solution focus and finding.*

Classic change management approaches are based on problem-solving mindsets. They start by asking, "What's the problem?" When you do that, you focus your energy on what you want less of and you try to "fix" things. This does not lead to new knowledge, but re-creates the processes you study. Indeed, when you solve one problem, we tend to seek the next one in line. While doubtlessly productive, the problem-focus approach makes people defensive and blames givers rather than being creative and generative. Problem solving pushes you to seek the negative and creates a tendency either to search for flaws or to defend yourself from those who identify flaws within the areas of your responsibility.

Those focusing on the positive, in this context, may often be viewed with suspicion or apprehension. These positive contributors are frequently seen as unrealistic, idealistic, lacking in critical thinking, adversarial promoters, or at the worst, propagandists.

Problem solving mindset is the best way to maintain status quo and current solutions since you start and remain in a static frame of what "the world is today." You begin with a model or an ideal based on what you know now.

The most powerful force for change is a new idea. So you want to move away from a problem-solving mindset. The meetings tools used in the REFRESHING change process create new images, models, ideas, and knowledge. They are solution-finding mindset meetings.

Problems may be identified, especially in terms of the present and current reality, but once they have been noted, the group moves to developing an ideal future scenario. You become a "naïve dreamer," as some problem-solving addicts say.

Actually, you capture the best of the past in order to build the best into the future. You study what works well. The problem-focus approach enables organisations to improve existing structures. Solution focus enables participants to build a long-term vision and a strong commitment to fulfilling that vision. You take participants from a "discovery" of their best, through a "visioning/dreaming" of better, the "design" necessary to get there, and finally to the "delivery" of an action plan or the step to get moving. It is about looking at what works and determining how to do more of what works. When you do more of what works, the stuff that doesn't work goes away! This is almost heresy to our problem-solving mindset.

1.8.   Q. CHANGE TAKES TIME, AND YOU NEVER REALLY KNOW WHEN IT'S FINISHED, SINCE IT'S ABOUT CHANGING PEOPLE. SO HOW CAN YOU ENSURE 'HIGH SPEED' THROUGH THE **REFRESHING** CHANGE PROCESS?

First, lets recall the steps of the REFRESHING change management process:
(1) Small-scale solutions and versions of the change; (2) vision of the change; (3) letting go of the old and doing new everyday actions; (4) sponsored projects; and (5) burning bridges thanks to processes and culture.

The REFRESHING change management process *is a faster way to implement a change than the classic change management approaches*.

In classic change management methods, leaders typically make the assumption that they can mandate the pace of change despite its complexity or people's readiness or stamina. They often believe that the transformation must be made immediately. But when these leaders establish and sustain high-pressure conditions inappropriately, employee morale usually drops, resistance rises, and implementation flounders, all of which slows down the change effort. Based on their experience of this unavoidable sequence, these same leaders believe that the best way to speed things up is to skip or abbreviate steps in the change management process or to avoid dedicating enough time for a step to create commitment.

Actually, they could do the steps of the change management process more quickly if they did them differently, using the tools of the REFRESHING change management process.

Moreover, the REFRESHING change management process is *a high-speed process, thanks to several levers:*

- You don't have to re-launch the change.
- There is an obsession for action, not for conceptual thinking or for "shoulds" speeches.
- Commitment ensures speed. For example, you do not waste time fighting against resistance.
- Involvement of a large and diverse group of people, ensures quality and speed.

1.8.1.   Q. What do you mean by 'You don't have to re-launch the change'?

The REFRESHING change management process speeds up the change process by ensuring that change management is *done just once, and fully*. This is achieved because people are rendered committed.

The process ensures that we take the time to invest in engaging the organisation from the very beginning of the design of the what and how of the change. This is not what happens in classic methods: the change is officially done as people often pretend to have changed; they change superficially; or they change as long as somebody is watching over them. So either you believe the smoke screen, or if you don't, you try to do the management of change again and again! Let's not kid ourselves. With the current way we manage change, and its failure rate of 70 to 80 percent, whatever time we think we dedicate to it, we probably need to start the change over again and again. Or we give up after having tried it for a while. Talk about a waste of time and a slow process!

1.8.2.   *Q. What do you mean by 'There is an obsession for action not conceptual thinking or shoulds'?*

The REFRESHING process *is not about speeches but about results.*

The first obsession is to *set the conditions for actions.* The process speeds up change management by positively impacting people's commitment, readiness, and ability to act. This is done by applying the principle "go slow to go fast." You invest time to set them up for action in the beginning of the change process and in each of its tools. This investment always brings a significant return in speeding up the planning and people's willingness to act. Let's not forget that what is key in change management is the speed of achieving the results of the actions to change, not of the number of steps of the change roadmap or their length! For example, attention to step 1 is the most powerful of all action acceleration strategies. For leaders, it speeds up the change management process by enabling them to hasten the process of gathering and coalescing existing information and opinions about the theme that prompts the need for change. It also greatly enhances the quality of the information gathered. Without a clear and relevant picture of what is known, of who has been doing what and what the current reactions are, attempting to lead to change is slow and plagued by back and forth movements.

The second obsession is to *do things only if they prompt concrete acts*. During all steps of the process, the meeting tools prompt concrete actions, big or small, that, de facto, implement or initiate the change. A big difference with classic change management approaches is that with the REFRESHING change management process, there is not "first communication and then action." Instead, action occurs at every step of the process. Central conceptual and high-level planning time is reduced. You focus on actions. Step 1, for example, is all about action. Step 2 is about defining a federating idea that supports actions, which is often started before the end of step 1. It is a bit like a "ready-fire-aim!" orientation, which is always counter-balanced by continuous learning and course correction actions that then nurture the next actions. It enables us always to start a small act of change in a concrete manner while in parallel fine-tuning the design and implementation of it progressively. So design and implementation of change are done in parallel and accelerate each other.

1.8.3.   *Q. What do you mean by 'Commitment ensures speed'?*

The REFRESHING change management process speeds up the change process by *avoiding the need to spend your time* telling people to do stuff, trying to convince them, fighting their resistance, or trying to make them look for solutions instead of problems.

For example, barriers to the flow of information and new ideas are lowered as people forge links with others. This is another waste of time that is avoided by meetings that enable action taking.

And, the *commitment makes people want to implement changes* in their day-to-day context—yet another thing you do not need to spend time trying to convince them to do.

1.8.4.   *Q. What do you mean by 'Involvement of a large amount of, and varied, people ensures quality, thus, ensures speed'?*

A great idea just doesn't become a great idea. You get a great idea by having a lot of good ideas on the table. A great idea is a compounding effect of a lot of good ideas. The right kind of collaboration enabled by the meeting tools of the REFRESHING change process will drastically improve the quality of the ideas being shared. The more people you bring into a room and get around the table, the higher your odds of getting great ideas.

For example, the amount of time involved in developing a plan the right way the first time pales in comparison to the time and effort required to correct and resurrect a stalled plan devised in secret or without those who have information to make the plan relevant.

So the REFRESHING change management process speeds up the change by using broad involvement to ensure informed and qualitative design and implementation of the solutions embedded in a change.

The benefits of broad involvement ultimately outweigh the perceived costs of involving a large amount of people. In the meeting tools of the REFRESHING change management process, a large group of people are involved, and there is a mix that represents the whole organisation. The worst-case scenario, but a frequent one when you use classic change management approaches, is that decisions about the change are made quickly by a few people who then ask that it be executed by all. This is true for top-down, bottom-up, or silo versions of the classic approaches. About halfway through the execution time, you find out that most of the people have no idea what you're talking about, and have no idea about how to get it done. So you have to loop back. You do a lot of communication, pressuring those openly expressing lack of understanding, and you believe that now everybody is on board. Most often, you have to redesign the solutions embedded in the change.

The meeting tools used in the REFRESHING change management process enable you to *immediately involve a critical mass of people*, and thus access a critical mass of information that enriches decisions about the change. With everyone in the room, you do not have to go out of the room to get information, so you do not need to postpone change because you need a little more information. The decisions you make are informed ones.

The common belief in organisations is that speed is served by making changes with fewer people in the decision-making process. The fact of the matter is that *no decisions are good decisions if they're not understood or implemented in the real world.*

Meeting tools of the REFRESHING change management process help you do both. What is more, you will actually need less total meeting time across your organisation since all people are regrouped during fewer meetings and thus a shorter period of time. During the meetings, people from all levels and functions, along with customers, suppliers, and important others, contribute to the solution and the planning of actions. You avoid myopic views and solutions when designing the change. Indeed, the different parts of the organisation stop resolving systemic issues from their own myopic perspective because they are now in direct and physical contact with the people who hold the perspective of the other components of the whole. Actions and decisions that result from these meetings are rooted in the concrete realities of the people and based on what works. Moreover, there is wider access to information and the information is used purposefully. The people who are closest to the solutions have critical information that enriches the search for solutions embedded in the change. And those who bring the data react to what is concluded or proposed based on this data.

Finally, *learning and creativity can occur* when people are committed because they take the risk to examine their assumptions and are open to feedback—yet another source of qualitative decisions. Because the organisation is well represented in the meeting room, decisions and actions occur rapidly, with little time spent waiting around or selling an idea of change.

All this enhances the probability that the defined change is the right thing to do and implemented in the best possible way.

Slim Lambert

I disagree. As mentioned, the REFRESHING change management process makes *change management initiative an intrinsic part of running the business and delivering product and services.*

For example, step 1 nurtures itself from business as usual or day-to-day issues. People only address things that are important for them and relevant to their everyday work life. Step 1 is rooted in the "real world," and serves as basis for the rest of the steps of the change management process. So the risk of creating a parallel world through the change management initiative is low. Real business issues are addressed because people are empowered to address the things they want inside a frame defined by the theme. Don't forget that although people are asked to address a theme, they are asked and given the real opportunity to work on things they find important inside that theme. They instinctively equate "important" with "it has an impact on their day-to-day life in the job." *You can't get more close to "real" issues than that!*

Moreover, you can trust the leader defines a theme that is linked to running the business and delivering product and services.

It is true that people have to dedicate some time to attend meetings. So the day-to-day activities are stopped during that time. To do what? Meetings! They will do meetings anyway. The ones of the REFRESHING change management process are just more focused on actions and structured differently compared to regular meetings.

Moreover, as with any meeting, nothing stops the organisation from being creative to avoid hampering the regular activities of the business. No employee works twenty-four hours a day and seven days a week anyway (see the point?).

Q. Is it not dangerous to be 'involving' when you drive a change? For example, won't there be lack of strategic direction of the change since everybody is involved in planning local change actions?

First, lets recall the steps of the REFRESHING change management process:
(1) Small-scale solutions and versions of the change; (2) vision of the change; (3) letting go of the old and doing new everyday actions; (4) sponsored projects; and (5) burning bridges thanks to processes and culture.

As I stated earlier, *when you involve those who will need to implement the change, the new solution embedded in the change is more qualitative. So the risk lies in not involving people.*

In the REFRESHING change management process, people are engaged up front and are a part of generating the tactical plans for a change. As I have said, this does not mean opening up the strategic direction of the change to a company-wide consensus process. It doesn't mean you let anyone ignite an initiative from any level in the organisation. It is not a simple bottom-up approach to change management. All actions are defined inside the frame of the theme proposed by the leader. This theme is a translation of the strategic direction the leader wants to give. The energy and commitment of the people are channelled and framed.

When people are invited to help solve tough business problems and have a big impact on the results, they become inspired, motivated, and committed. They pride themselves in being able to deliver results that serve the whole organisation, unlike with the current lack of empowerment of people in organisations, So sometimes, because they are truly involved and empowered, they see an opportunity to prove to management that their ideas generate results if they are involved.

Involvement also creates commitment to the change because it *gives employees some control over the change*. When we humans choose for ourselves, we are far more committed to the outcome, almost by a factor of five to one. Conventional approaches to change management underestimate the return on this kind of investment. And the outcome is something people have to live with and defend in front of peers and their bosses, because it is they who proposed the outcome. You therefore benefit from the immense energy embedded in people's need of being congruent

Thanks to the specificities of the meeting tools used in the REFRESHING change management process, everybody, not just the senior executives, *is given a lengthy lead time* when a change is proposed. They know about the change before it happens. It enables them to digest it, go through the sorrow curve to build a sense of ownership of the answer and a feeling of belonging that ensures everybody is in the same boat.

This insight building, made possible thanks to the involvement of all, creates commitment

1.9.2. *Q. Is the desire to involve all impacted by the change a sign that those in charge of the organisation lack leadership or smarts?*

No, definitely no. On the contrary, it is a sign of great leadership and organisational functioning acumen. No one can do it alone, especially when you need to reinvent an organisation in the context of change. Significant change needs a critical mass of powerful empowered teams that design, implement, and drive the change. No leader, regardless of talent, should single-handedly develop the vision and strategy for a change effort. Even if the leader is capable of developing a grand vision and a well-crafted strategic plan, the more important issue here is its implementation. And the leader is not the one who will implement it. It is the people of the organisation.

The best and the brightest minds can produce brilliant strategies, but without an agile, flexible, engaged organisation willing to implement them, the strategies are useless. People at all levels of the organisation need to care about the change, take ownership of it, and want to implement it despite difficulties and hurdles that are inherent to anything that is new.

So there is no choice but to involve the maximum number of people in the change process.

At least a critical mass, if not all, of the people in the organisation need to be involved in developing the what and the how of a change. These include all its key internal and external stakeholders.

The number of people involved goes beyond what leaders or stakeholders accustomed to the classic change management approaches probably think is prudent or possible. This is not because they do not see the benefit, lack courage, or are not smart. They just probably have not witnessed or heard about the meeting tools that make this possible and that are used in the REFRESHING change management process.

People involved need to have the opportunity to make suggestions and decisions, take responsibility for their actions, and commit to implementing change actions according to their position within the organisation.

They need to have the opportunity to influence decisions—the design, implementation, and designing a change—if you want them to be relevant, implementable, and sustainable.

The leader should actively elicit involvement from all the people who will implement directly or indirectly the change.

In sociological terms, critical mass is defined as that group necessary for an idea to be adopted by the whole population.

Critical mass is sometimes said to range between 10 and 40 percent of a population. Do not to get fixated on an absolute number. Instead, remember the key concept of representation of the whole organisation. Any number is okay, as long as collectively you have enough "weight to the snowball" of support, which grows as it rolls forward effectively toward the change. Keep in mind that people with far-reaching position power or charisma may be less influential than those in small, somewhat removed pockets in the organisation. Getting the "movers and shakers" to support your change effort, regardless of their role, is key to your success. Be sure also to identify those who hold the relevant information, whatever their position in the organisation. Try to involve "positive deviants" that have already tried out parts of the solution embedded in the change successfully or learned as they tried to do so.

Remember you can organise parallel meetings during the same period of time. This accelerates the creation of a critical mass.

1.9.4. *Q. So the selection of who is involved in each meeting is based on the principle of having the whole system present in the meeting. Can you elaborate a bit on why it is key to have the 'whole system'?*

By whole system, I mean all the stakeholders who have an interest in the theme or a possibility to act to design or implement a change focused on the theme.

It is a cross-section of as many interested parties as practical. A way of scoping the whole is to identify the people who have authority, resources, expertise, information, and need in the context of the purpose of the meeting.

1.9.5.   *Q. Why is having the whole represented or present important?*

As mentioned *it is linked to the way complex systems function.*

Exploring the whole before acting on any part also *renders people better able to contain their anxiety about differences and roadblocks.* They experience themselves living on the same planet, facing similar constraints, with the same issues to resolve. You want to make the whole organisation visible for all through the visibility of the interests, concerns, and opinions during meetings. Most of us only understand best our own jobs and the work groups of which we are a part. This is true for all, even for the leaders. It would not be fair to expect the contrary. It is normal that most people are ignorant of the larger system in which they work. When a need for change arises, an unawareness of how things work in the larger system would lead to short sightedness and suboptimal solutions. Issues would be resolved in favour of one work group, unit, or organisational silo. This would make a change non-sustainable and its embedded solution of poor quality. *When the whole system is visible*, people understand how the work that precedes theirs enables them to do their job effectively and how their job affects the work of those whose contribution comes next. People become committed to collaborating in order to achieve common goals that best serve the total organisation and its customers, not just their own functions or work groups. People learn how to move forward together as a unified community, and above all else, to accept joint responsibility for their common purpose. All this helps people think beyond their existing frameworks. At the same time, it encourages people to consider the concrete realities that must be addressed if their local change plans are to produce tangible results. *They can't possibly understand its subtleties unless they hear the perspectives of others in the whole system.*

Moreover, the best way to *generate creativity is diversity*. And maximum diversity comes from a representation of the whole system.

Finally, it is only through giving people a chance to have their say, feel as though they have been heard, and ideally find common ground for the future that they will be engaged and committed to action. And you need all the people!

So building relationships among stakeholders who don't normally communicate is essential to effective implementation of change actions.

Be aware—you want the whole system present. But you also want anybody who wants to participate to be allowed to do so. When participation in the process is *voluntary*, it reinforces the idea that everyone has something to contribute. Even those who might be opposed to the idea underlying the change, those who might be losing something because if the change is implemented, and the sceptics and cynics all must be given a chance to speak up.

The process to select participants starts off with leaders proposing a scope for the whole.

However, the mindset to adopt is one in which the leader is not the only one who handpicks all the participants nor the only one who holds the truth about the scope of the whole. So you use a selection process that gives equal opportunity for everyone to participate and invite those they feel should participate. *The leader picks a starting point* in each section of the map of the whole. You then ask each starting point for two or three names that fit the criteria defined below. You then ask each of the new names to give you two or three names that fit the same criteria. *After one, two, or three iterations the same names should appear.* That's when you stop the selection process and select from the total short list. Your final list of participants is based on their desire to participate.

The criteria identifying and short-listing who should be invited are:

- Who's voice needs to be heard?
- Who has information that will be needed to create effective solutions?
- Who will be directly or indirectly affected by the changes that are being considered?
- Whose additional perspectives might contribute valuable insights?

- Who could receive real benefit by being a part of the conversation?
- Who has unique or different perspectives to offer?
- Who has the authority to implement potential changes and ultimately approve the changes being recommended?
- Who has the responsibility for the outcomes and operational responsibility for the proposed changes?
- Who is likely to be opposed to the new course of action? Invite them!
- Who will ensure the change will be focused outward?

A comment about this—all changes must either serve an external client, partner, or somebody who is a key stakeholder. I believe that changes that just make internal life easier for people in the organisation should not be given priority. Current and potential clients of the organisation should be at the centre or be key members of the meeting tools. They have key information to share. External stakeholders bring important insights and are often the major impetus for driving change. They also break up internal collusions and remind the organisation of its larger purpose. Aim for 25 to 40 percent of participants at a meeting to be outside stakeholders. The exact number is not important. Very likely, they already know your problems. Customers appreciate being involved and being at the centre of the change. They will be thankful for having been invited into the conversation and help you ensure the sustainability of the change.

No. All of the energy of one leader or a couple of leaders could not get several thousand people into motion. *These people are the only ones who can get themselves in motion*, in a sustainable manner.

The leaders still make the final decisions about major change actions, participate in meetings, and frame the change according to the theme they propose at step 1.

The shaping of the design and implementation of the change is generated throughout the organisation. Each person is asked to step up and lead his or her portion of the change effort. *Leaders help people take the leadership of the change.* Leadership impact is not about how aggressive, decisive, and visionary you are. It is about how you bring that out in others. As a rule of thumb, the higher you move in your leadership levels, the more important it becomes to understand the value of sharing of power. Leadership and active participation by leaders is crucial—but not sufficient—to ensure successful change. Leaders build support among the people who will need to convert a vision of change into a new reality. Otherwise, *the change starts and ends at the top.* If leading change were nothing more than an intellectual exercise in rearranging structures and redesigning processes, our lives would be a lot simpler. Leading people in a new direction is about acting to let them reshape their view of the world, voluntarily through self-discovery of the what and how of the change.

It is about empowering them to shatter their sense of stability, toss out their old standards of success, and shatter their status quo voluntarily through self-discovery. And then it is about empowering them to replace what they've shattered with a new, coherent, and energizing vision of what they believe the future can and should be. This is achieved using the REFRESHING change management process. Do not forget the process set the environment and then a lot of the work is self-managed by the people. Change brings instability, upheaval, and uncertainty. To the individuals involved, change also means new job requirements, new bosses, new reporting structures, new performance standards, new compensation plans, and new patterns of power, influence, and control, and, consequently, high-stakes office politics. Any of these things are enough to keep most of us awake at night. It cannot be done without the people who will face all this, and it cannot be imposed on them.

1.10.1. *What are the other actions of the leader?*

A successful organisation depends on leadership.

As mentioned, *to drive a change, you need a specific type of leadership*. These leaders do not give the answers. They may have a vision about a change embedded in the selection of the theme. But the actual solutions about how best to meet the themes' challenges have to be made by the people closest to the action. The most important action of leaders is to define the theme. It embeds the challenges that need to be addressed differently, without insisting on specific solutions. I will detail this in the following chapters.

Leaders also *ensure that the REFRESHING change management process is implemented.* They create its enabling conditions. They will probably need to withstand the pull of the organisation to act in more traditional ways, which can sabotage democratic-like principles. They must relinquish the job of chief discoverer to the people. Leaders ensure that people and management stay with uncertainty. They ensure that people do not abandon the change management process at the first moment of fear. They ensure that people do not fall back to what is safe and sure and that people support the principles underlying the change management process in the midst of chaos, confusion, and even conflict. Leaders probably should be prepared for these sort of risks when their initial efforts to empower the organisation are met with such distrust. These risks reflect people's feelings of betrayal and insult based on past change management. Finally, leaders need to encourage managers to free up team members' time. It is often the first line of management that has the greatest reluctance to give their staff the autonomy and time for implementing change actions. They often perceive any risk of loss of control, authority, and power as a threat. Role modelling by leaders is key here.

During the meeting tools of the REFRESHING change management process, leaders are regular participants. Straight talk is, therefore, key. They need to provide all the available facts, their thoughts and feelings about those facts, and what they would like to have happen. And even more importantly, rather than fulfilling the expectation for answers, leaders have to ask the tough questions. Rather than protecting people from an outside threat, they have to let people feel the pinch of reality. Rather than quelling conflict, they have to draw the issues out. Rather than maintaining norms, they have to challenge "the way we do business." They need to resist the temptation to reaffirm authority by quick fixes and moving on an issue too quickly. They need to resist preempting followers from sharing the stress, understanding the full dimensions of the challenges, and coming forward with solutions from the ranks.

What is key is that leaders let go of the beliefs that one cannot manage or lead what one cannot control. They need to drive and facilitate the opportunities that enable, those that will change, to be involved, and commit to the change and the design of its what and how of the change. The scope of a leader's influence actually increases when they let go of the control belief. They do not just produce a few champions of the change but hundreds of them.

The second belief they need to let go of is the one that *the leader is the one who has a vision and convinces people to trust and follow him or her toward a change through his or her charisma or smarts.* This is an archetype of a leader being a hero or heroine who envisions things nobody else does. It is also the archetype of a leader being so sure about his or beliefs that he or she has the right to jeopardize the capacity to deliver of the whole organisation. Well, is just that an archetype at best, if not a fallacy. Of course, you might argue that this hero is not alone but surrounded by a select few. The fallacy remains the same. It is just applied to more people! The truth is that those who will implement the change or who need to change do not believe in such heroes. And if they do they do not do it for long. Moreover, they do not believe that these selected few are representative of them and their interests, values, concerns, or day-to-day knowledge of how things are done. Of course, this has nothing to do with the intrinsic value of the selected few. It is just that business life is too complex.

After reading the book you, I hope that you will agree that *as a leader of a change, the following assumptions are unfounded:*

- Unless I keep a tight rein, I cannot control the outcomes.
- The REFRESHING change management process means that I must completely let go of any influence or control.
- I will have to completely abdicate my authority, responsibility, and ability to provide input based on my knowledge and experience.
- I will be excluded from the process of designing the change and its implementation.
- We must keep a firewall between the organisation and its stakeholders.
- If we include outsiders in our change process, we will be airing our dirty laundry in public, thus alienating the very people who are necessary to our success.
- Those affected by a change will not build ownership and commitment within the organisation and with those outside. People resist change.
- Involving customers and suppliers working with us to build a future will not make them invested in our success, make them become true partners in the change process, or move them from making demands to offering ideas for mutual gain.
- Productivity will suffer if I involve a lot of people.

- The majority cannot be trusted to put the organisation's interests first. Self-interest will take over.
- Even if people understand all the issues and the role they and their departments play, they will not be willing to offer ideas and make decisions that benefit the whole more than themselves.
- People will not be able to understand the issues and opportunities facing the organisation, the stakeholders, or even their own mid-term ones.
- People do not want to be offered the opportunity to be involved in making difficult decisions; they want these decision thrust on them to avoid taking responsibilities for their own destiny.
- Changes designed by the best and the brightest are cost-effective.
- The leader and those the leader chooses are the only ones capable of determining the appropriate course of action.

Slim Lambert

2. STEP 1

At this step, the leader has identified a business need or a concern that will require either finding a new solution or changing current solutions. This is the *theme*. The *what* and *how* are not yet defined. Sure, the leader probably has an intuition, but he or she is smart enough not to believe he or she alone has the answer or can implement it just by "selling" it to those who need to implement it.

2.1. WHAT ARE THE OBJECTIVES OF THIS STEP?

It is to empower people to build themselves the elements of the equation that defines the success factors that will build their commitment to local change actions to address the theme.

The change equation is: $C = De + Ds + S + Co + B$. It states that change (C) will occur when:

- There is desire (De) for change, that is, people have been awakened to the need, and want to change. This awakening needs to be done by self-discovery.
- There is a vision of a better and feasible local desired state (Ds) of one's day-to-day activities, in the context of a shared common ground of the group to which one feels one belongs.

Making the desired state a reality requires a new solution embedded in the change. This is done with a sense of belonging the whole organisation.

- There are small steps (S) implemented or planned to implement the desired states.
- There is congruence (Co), that is, honouring and being proud of things of one's past and being convinced that the past is being used as the foundation for building the local desired states.
- There is a belief (B) that the new and as yet unknown ways of doing things will be relevant, that they'll truly be states one should desire locally, and that no part of an organisation can survive or succeed in isolation to reach these desired states.

2.1.1. *What are the outputs of step 1 of the REFRESHING change management process that create desire for change?*

Desire could be understood in several ways. Other ways of framing desire for change are:

- awakening to a better status quo;
- identifying operational targets of the change;
- reframing of the *as is.* (Reframing is not so much doing away with old ways, as building a new and exciting future. It is looking at the as is in a different way, thereby reframing its entire meaning to something that needs to be changed.)

- identifying levers for a better solution or desired state;
- identifying disconfirming evidence that the belief that the status quo is the best option;
- self-discovery of evidence that other ways of doing things are better enough to launch a change;
- willingness to change;
- unfreezing of perceptions;
- exposing and creating a need for local change actions;
- surfacing dissatisfaction with and envisioning of alternatives to the current ways of doing things;
- insight and "aha" moments regarding the theme.
- awakening to the fact that several local operational or business-as-usual issues can be better addressed through one change program;
- inquiry followed by action and exploring further into certainties about the current ways of doing things;
- shaking up of people's comfort zone;
- defining the business case for a change in the form of local change action plans;
- building feelings of a need to change, an urgency for change, and interest in addressing the theme.

When first meeting a leader who has a vision about implementing a change, I'm sometimes asked, "If the solution or the change is explained well, is that not enough?"

The answer is no. *People become committed to a change only if they are empowered and involved in the design of the what and how of the change.* They won't desire the change otherwise. To create the awakening, people need to believe that a change is critical, before even being motivated to contribute to the change. The awakening then becomes a clear sense of urgency. While a concrete business case may be necessary, alone it is not enough; people first have to discover, see, and then feel the need to change. This is only possible through true empowerment and involvement. It is not possible with classic change management approaches, however good you are at it!

A common scenario in the classic approaches is that the leader has already begun planning the tactical implementation of the change. Most leaders are quick to devote time, energy, and resources to planning. But little if any energy is spent preparing people in the organisation for change. You've probably heard a leader say something like, "This is the direction we are going in, and you just need to accept it and move on." Rarely does this approach result in lasting change or even in a change. You give those individuals who resist the change a solid platform from which to recruit others—who would have been supporters if the proper change management process had been used. Organisations are not a thing to be operated on. Organisations are people. Do not forget that organisations are open and complex systems, composed of complex components: people.

So, awakening people to the need for a change requires that you *help the organisation to discover* some clear local and perhaps global goals to which most people can aspire. This is done in the step 1 meeting tool.

Awakening happens when people are convinced that they worked together to make the change, that the organisation changed itself. *Awakening is pulled out of people.*

You might ask, If the awakening is not pushed by the leader, who sets the stage? The people themselves set the stage during step 1 of the change management process. People discover the why of the change, as well as the why now. And they immediately propose the what and the how of the local change. This makes them discover the organisation's future—the where to. Then, they discover the personal benefits of the change—what's in it for me? All this needs to be done through self-discovery because change requires a redefinition of who we are and what we do. *This cannot be imposed.*

Awakening requires that people accept to twist their past success if they are obstacles for their immediate future. It's highly emotional. It requires capitalising on the energy of positive and negative emotions. This is done during step 1 meeting tool.

Step 1 is the foundation for the future change behaviours and ways of working. This means changing people's perceptions of what is possible. It also means *awakening them to their own perceptions*.

Awakening requires that people discover and build by themselves the arguments for the change being needed. However, *awakening is coupled with the design of a solution*. This coupling ensures interest, commitment, and familiarity with the solution embedded in a change. The problem is accepted, and the solution is understood because people understand its origin, its purpose, and the means to implement it. After all, it was they who discovered all this!

However, it is not just the awakening of a few. *It is the awakening of a critical mass.*

A critical mass is moved from *pre-contemplation to contemplation.* The pre-contemplation stage of individual change is often the most difficult stage to break out of on the journey to create lasting changes. Pre-contemplation is the time before people realise that change has to happen. They are stuck in pre-change ways of doing things. They may even be happy there, or they don't believe they are capable of changing the current situation. They are not even considering the idea of changing. People all have to pass through this stage on their way to the active stage of contemplation, preparation, and action.

Contemplation is the time when people are committed to changing in the near future. They start thinking that they need to make a change. They desire a change. Maybe they started to feel emotional about their situation and saw ways to make it better. Maybe others started pointing out a need for change, and they began to agree with them. Maybe the "positive deviants" they will learn to get to know during step 1 demonstrated convincingly that one can do things differently and have (more) success.

A comment about emotions, change, and awakening: becoming emotional is a great way to change quickly. Unfortunately, in the pre-contemplation stage, people do not have any emotion about their current situation. The motivation to change has to come from the outside. Some outside influence has to act as the trigger that motivates them to begin the change process. Be aware, the trigger is not the solution embedded in the change. Indeed, at the pre-contemplation stage, people filter and rationalise data that proves the need for a change. For example, there is quite a bit of evidence to suggest that people know that smoking, taking drugs, and eating a steady diet of ice-cream and burgers is bad for them. But they do it anyway, so education isn't an effective way to create change. It is a trigger for self-discovery of the solution embedded in the change. The connections and interactions created in step 1 meeting tool are the external triggers needed.

Facts and figures won't get the job done to create readiness for change. It's necessary to build it on an emotional level too. In the step 1 meetings, this is enabled thanks to true dialogue and storytelling with representatives of the whole organisation and stakeholders. It enables a rare experience that is a bit like having an executive experiencing responsibility for the complaint desk and field employees experiencing involvement in strategic decision-making. However, thanks to the structure of the meetings, as they live and discover the disaster scenarios, people are immediately given the means and opportunities to build the solutions. This avoids falling into denial or becoming paralyzed by fear. It moves people into at least the contemplation if not the planning stage. People are guided to conclude that change is essential and that they can do and want to do something about it at their local level.

To awaken people, you do not try to convince them that the current ways of doing things are not the right ones. *You make them envision a different future without criticizing the current one.* This creates a spontaneous disengagement and dissatisfaction with the present and the past. You awaken them to a local vision of the change needed for the theme.

The vision for the applicable-to-all change occurs in step 2 of the change process. Why? We talked about the need do to so in order to ensure commitment and a qualitative vision at step2. Put simply it is to create the interest toward the applicable-to-all change at the start of step 2! The need for people to be *truly* interested in changing is often underestimated. At the start of step 2, people will be asking for the applicable-to-all change because it will enable them to be congruent with what they've done and committed to in step 1. They will be interested in the vision proposed in step 2, both emotionally and intellectually. So step 2 will be easy, quick, and not plagued by lack of commitment. Step 1 enables people to discover and live the aha moments of what's in it for them to change locally in the interest of an applicable-to-all change. After the wake-up calls have been created by enough people in the step 1 meeting tools to mobilize action, the change process is underway, and officially begins in step 2 for the whole organisation with the definition of a vision for an applicable-to-all change. Step 1 makes the need for a local and global applicable-to-all change apparent to the entire organisation. Step 1 will identify and deliver concrete examples of what the change could look like, and its benefits. Basically what you do in step 1 is to say, "We will let you discover by yourself if there is a need for change and what that change is for you."

There is also an awakening of people not present in the step 1 meeting. Participants come out of the step 1 meeting tool committed to deliver their plan for a change. *They realise they have to change or convince bosses and peers of the need to change.* This is included in the action plan designed during the meetings.

Step 1 meeting tool enables the *acceleration of unlearning without having to spend a long time accumulating knowledge.* Those who will need to change are encouraged and have the opportunities to find the knowledge they need during the meeting, so they can put it into action in order to find solutions to address the theme. There isn't a necessity for them to remember this knowledge or to be the holders of it. That wouldn't be realistic anyway in today's world. The meeting empowers and enables people to access all kinds of information, beliefs, and experiences that are inside other people present at the meeting—and to apply this information and knowledge as soon as they acquire it.

Step 1 enables to give people *the necessary time to understand and digest the need for change.* But this is not just an intellectual game. After all, what would make us think that these people are so much smarter than the leaders that they do not need time, intuition, the aha moment, data and probably advice to develop insight? The people are given the opportunity to walk through the same inquiry and discovery process as the leader before proposing the theme. Thanks to the step 1 meeting tool, people will often do it even more extensively, more in depth, and with more sources of information. They are also given the opportunity to influence the outcome of the discovery process. This enables them to better scope the global applicable-to-all change to be launched in step 2. So awakening is a coupled with a sense of ownership by people toward the local changes they can implement.

Slim Lambert

Is there not a risk that step 1 creates paralysis by analysis? No, because the output is action and an action plan implementable locally. Understanding and digestion are done through the implementation of local change actions. Moreover, organisational change, when you get right down to it, boils down to persuading massive numbers of people to stop doing what they've been doing for years and to start doing something they probably don't want to do—at least not at first. Recognition of the necessity of change and doing the diagnosing by the people themselves are crucial first steps. *That is well worth allowing them a bit of time and space for some analysis!*

To summarize, awakening and the desire to change locally is key because we can't expect people to jump in the river just because the leader assures them it's a good idea.

This is summarized in the change equation is: $C = De + Ds + S + C + B$.

Common ground is the agreed area that will be focused on after the step 1 meeting tool. It could be a brief statement as to what these areas cover. More often, it is an action plan. Common ground does not mean compromise or conflict resolution. At this step of the change management process, you need to consider conflict as healthy and as important information, not something to be resolved or suppressed.

Common ground and beliefs are what energise people. It is often the core of the global and applicable-to-all change that will be defined in step 2. People are pulled into focusing on the future and common ground rather than previous problems and conflicts. Nothing is swept under the rug, but problems and conflicts are considered as information, not action agenda items.

When I say common ground, I am not assuming that consensus within the community does or should exist at all times. If consensus does occur, it is an added bonus, but we do not strive for it. You suggest people not try to change each other's minds and not work to reconcile opposites, only to admit their existence. You encourage people to express their differences so that everybody knows where they stand. You neither avoid nor confront the extremes. Rather, you put our energy into staking out the widest common ground on which all can stand. You urge people to resist compromise so that a shared perception of genuine common ground can emerge. You establish common ground perceptions of shared dilemmas, experiences, world views, trends, and so on.

Why are conflicts not resolved? Step 1 meetings create the conditions under which commonalities take precedence and diversity is appreciated. The meeting quickly establishes and enlarges the ground for agreement and cooperation, essentially eliminating any danger that conflict will get out of hand. So people can speak freely and argue for their points of view, knowing that a true dialogue takes place against a backdrop of solid common ground.

The prospect of assembling a large group of strong-willed and vocal people and turning them loose to argue can seem daunting. But remember that people behave differently in different circumstances. Participants discover shared aspirations, values, and direction that would be enabled by the change. Most of us have been in meetings where you spend a great deal of time and energy, trying to force people to a consensus that shatters as the parties go their own ways after the meeting. In the step 1 meeting tool, and in other meeting tools, people are asked not to keep fretting over what is unresolved but rather to commit to what is possible now. If participants don't come to a spontaneous resolution in ten minutes or so, they are asked if they are ready to move the issue to the "not agreed" list. It is important to point out that the community ultimately decides whether this disagreement is substantive enough that one or two individuals from the conflicting parties temporarily leave the room to try to sort it out and see if the matter can be negotiated. If the parties return to the community empty-handed and still at odds with each other, the item is placed on a disagree list, and it ceases to be part of the discussion. At this point, the conflict is acknowledged and set aside. This simple mechanism can be used during any phase of the meeting tools.

People are told that a key feature of meetings tools is to act where people already agree. To focus relentlessly on unresolved issues reduces action planning time. This doesn't mean unagreed issues are dead forever. Parties often set aside time in the future to tackle them.

When significant differences arise in the meeting, the goal is not to negotiate a compromise or gain grudging agreement to support something with which some participants still basically disagree. Rather than spending a great deal of time and attention on a few items in conflict, the group can devote its energy to productive work.

The other benefit becomes that during the meeting tools people do not feel threats to their security or identity, since the focus of activity is always directed toward matters they accept and support.

People know there is a way, driven by them, to deal with conflict and strong emotions in a non-destructive manner. So instead of being dependent on a leader, people become dependable to each other to address the theme. Instead of succumbing to fight-flight group dynamics and becoming hostile or withdrawn, people become courageous and assertive. And since the way to resolve conflict is born out of the desire for productive work and an obsession for actions, instead of building castles in the air and resorting to wishful thinking or blind optimism, people become pragmatic and creative.

During the step 1 meeting tool, common ground is built by animation techniques such as time lines and the mind map.

Local desired states are created during the step 1 meetings. They often were not thought of before. Indeed, we ask people to share thoughts, move around, make their wishes known, and live with uncertainly. They experience a different version of realty than the one to which they are accustomed. They talk over issues they have not raised before with people they have never met. Many will take responsibility for matters they previously avoided or ignored. They identify what they really want. It is common, for example, that people voluntarily commit to actions made possible only because of the other people in the room. They are asked to look for solutions not problems. People change their capacity for action by experiencing themselves as part of a larger whole. All this enables you to define ambitious, realistic, and often unimagined local desired states when people are asked to define ideal future scenarios (five to twenty years out) rather than problem solving or conflict management. You elicit common hopes, fears, aspirations, and needs.

During step 1 meetings, people define the what and how of the desired states that are, in fact, probably local small versions of the global applicable-to-all change, which will be fine-tuned and defined in step 2. So you anchor the change that will be defined in step 2 in the concrete reality of people. They work on the desired states using elements from their everyday life, not from concepts, theories, or intuition. These desired states enable you to make a more relevant decision about the global applicable-to-all change during step 2 of the change process. You want people to find solutions for a theme. This of course can be called having a vision, but it is more of a concrete and *SMART objective that is the translation of the future applicable-to-all change* SMART is an acronym: specific, ambitious, measurable, agreed, reachable, time-bound. These objectives will lead to local desired states.

Desired states reached through SMART objectives are defined before the leader's vision for a change applicable to the whole organisation. Indeed this vision's main value and possible impact is to inspire and energise, not to define concrete day-to-day actions. The SMART objectives that define the local desired states are specific to a local context. People will implement them and the subsequent lessons learned are worth gold for a leader at step 2. People see the change proposed in step 2 as *their* change. It is, by definition, a quest, a dramatic stretch that energises and motivates the organisation to pursue different and exciting local change actions in the interest of the whole organisation and with knowledge of the organisation's constraints and resources. Metaphorically, this vision gives the picture of the future from the fifty-thousand-foot level. The vision is directional and inspirational, not necessarily tangible. *The local desired states defined in step 1 are the views of the future from the five-thousand-foot vantage point.* It is the organisation's best guess at what specific and local changes are required to accomplish or progress toward the vision of the global applicable-to-all change. It is still a picture of the future, but much more concrete.

During the step 1 meeting tool, people will have the opportunity to develop the best future state scenarios, test them, and determine which ones are the most likely to create an organisation that will, as a whole, successfully address the theme. You do not wait until the global applicable-to-all change has been defined to discover it is not compatible with local needs, requirements, constraints, and value-creating factors. Beyond the fact that is plain common sense, it avoids unnecessary cynicism, frustration of not being understood by those who will need to implement the change, and so on.

In a classic change management approach, we define a vision just to realise that it cannot be implemented locally or that it needs major adjustments. This is terrible for the credibility of the change effort and for the commitment of the people. It also wastes time on internal politics and resistance. *Announcing a new direction or vision does not make it become reality or even credible.* It does not make people commit to it. At best, people are not against it. For people to connect to it, they need time to chew on it, digest it, and make it their own. This cannot not occur through one-way conversations, great speeches, or even in Q&A sessions, none of which create enough interest and excitement to pull people from their comfort zones. They might say the idea is great and that others should change, but it's almost never enough for them to change.

Sometimes the desired states are radically different from the old way of doing things. So step 1 enables to test them before you proceed with a full-scale implementation to the whole organisation. *This is a complete opposite compared to the classic change management approach of defining a vision and then doing pilots.* The desired states are the people's, not the organisation's, current best guess about what will bring success locally and address the theme. Until your local desired outcomes are clear, people will not know why they should invest the effort it will take to support the change needed to address the theme proposed by the leader. When frontline employees and middle managers participate in creating the case for change, they add credibility to the assessment of need and leverage points for change and its impacts. Their empowerment to design and implement local change is a catalyst for their understanding and commitment. In step 2, the leaders will put all of this information into a clear picture applicable-to-all people of the organisation.

So, step 1 is already implementing a change to address the theme. It is about how each can participate in addressing the theme by doing what is doable where they work.

2.3. What are the outcomes of step 1 of the REFRESHING process that create the element of the change equation: 'the small steps to implement the desired states'?

As an output of the step 1 meeting you have:

- **Simultaneous change.**

Everybody moves forward at once, with their actions to change. This creates a momentum of small steps of action.

- **Empowerment.**

People have the knowledge of the complete organisation, which allows them to make decisions on their own of how to change locally in the benefit of the whole

- **An implementation follow-up team,** to support the REFRESHING change management process and to motivate everyone to follow up on their commitments made after step 1 meetings.

- **A list of actions that actually take place.**

This entails fast implementation of actions to reach a desired state that embed a new solution and change. They may not be perfect or exhaustive, but the energy and momentum is launched by the people through concrete actions, not just talks and speeches by the leaders.

- **Commitment.**

Everyone in the organisation supports the change efforts because they had been actively involved in the action planning and goal setting, and because they felt that their viewpoints and ideas had been heard. There is an engagement and enthusiasm for the need for change.

- **An abundance of new ideas and initiatives.**

There is an agreement on the key local areas that need change inside the theme and an agreed ambition in the form of an action plan to reach the desired states.

- Innovative **breakthroughs that can be best realised locally through the cooperation of different people of the organisation.**

During step 1 meetings, people do not just think and propose nice ideas. They create action plans and maintain the focus on what the future should be and what they and their peers can do. Step 1 becomes the founding block that defines the how and what of the global applicable-to-all change. Local action plans are defined by those who will need to change, based on the local meaning and impact of the global organisation's context and needs. *This is changing locally with the global organisation in mind. And when we say global, it is not just the company as a whole, but also the local stakeholders.* All action plans integrate the involvement or at least the support of the whole.

You prepare step 2 by creating routine, small-scale changes that when added together, *create the synergies and the critical mass that enable you to implement the global applicable-to-all change initiatives almost before having launched them.* You mainly sustain an existing commitment. Building something together is different from implementing someone else's ideas, and it is different from brainstorming possible solutions and then turning them over to someone else to implement. During step 1, people have the ability and opportunity to understand the environment in which they operate and the knowledge and insights necessary need to act locally in the best interest of the whole. Moreover, positive deviants come out the meeting with the blessing of the whole organisation to pursue and reinforce what they currently do that embeds the change.

Rather than having to choose between either substantial changes made in limited parts of an organisation or modest changes made across an entire organisation, step 1 of the change process makes it possible for substantial changes to be made across an entire organisation. They are substantial because each local change action is designed with the support of representatives of the whole organisation. And because step 1 meeting tools make it possible to bring together so many people at one time and in one place, substantial change can be made across entire organisation.

In step 1 meetings, leaders join other participants in various working groups and are as involved and accessible as anybody else in the room. This is an opportunity for the leader to fine-tune and prepare their vision of the change they will drive starting from step 2 of the change process. *After step 1 meeting tools, the big challenge for leaders is to channel this vast number of activities into the initiatives defined by the theme.* There is an unquestionable energy unleashed when people work collectively to bring their most desirable future into existence. Any change manager who uses the classic change management approaches would love to have that sort of a challenge! Actually, this channelling of local initiatives is not that daunting. Indeed, during the meetings that prompted these initiatives, people from different functions, levels, and locations in an organisation came together at the same time and place to plan and implement changes that they themselves have helped shape. So step 1 meetings actually provide a path to greater coordination, channelling, and integration of the different change initiatives across an entire organisation. It also ensures that individual efforts are aligned and consistent with the organisation's overall way to address the theme. However, this is not to say that all change must or does happen at once. The benefit of having changes occur simultaneously throughout an organisation is the achievement of leverage and synergy. Although some of these efforts may seem inconsequential on their own, collectively they result in a tremendously positive impact on an organisation. As mentioned, the role of the applicable-to-all change is not to "do" the change. It will have already started and been experimented with locally. It is to accelerate the change that is applicable to all.

Does that mean *the return on investment and the result of global applicable-to-all change is enhanced?* Yes. Its role is to create the new conditions that sustain the small changes that people have themselves identified and started to implement. The return on

Slim Lambert

investment and value-added of a global applicable-to-all change initiative are *taken to a whole new level*. It is not avoid resistance and hope to come close to the aimed performance that change should bring; it is rather to create a new *performance often greater than the one imagined by the leaders* when they had the intuition of a global applicable-to-all change.

Research indicates that performance increases slowly or rapidly at first, and then surges at a rapid rate until it bumps up against the operation's performance limits and flattens out. This is where the ambition of the global applicable-to-all change intervenes—to sustain and enhance, not to create.

There is historical record developed by the group. It is a testimony to their courage and survival skills. *It acknowledges that the past was not "only bad." It lends credibility to the directions and decisions taken in the past by the leader* as being "adapted to the context at the time." This, therefore, lends credibility to the future decisions and directions they will drive. Rather than being negative, it brings hope and confidence in people's ability to manage the future and the change that will create this future. It also defines a sense of continuity.

In addition, it pulls people to stop feeling connected to other people, who are identified with the old ways of doing things. This is a key. Indeed, we are a social species. We become and like to remain connected to those we know, to those who have taught us how to do things, and to those with whom we are familiar—even at times to our own detriment. If you ask people in an organisation to do things in a new way, as rational as that new way may seem to you, you will be setting yourself up against all that hard wiring, all those emotional connections they have toward those who taught them the old way.

Finally, not linking what you are doing today to what came before creates confusion and lack of congruence. *Human beings will do almost anything to maintain congruence.* The first thing they will do of course is to resist or attack the proposed need for change, its embedded solutions, since it is a threat to their congruence.

During step 1, the past is recognized and presented in a favourable light so letting go of it is easier. In addition, the next steps of the REFRESHING change process will reinforce this letting go of past action.

Change is a leap in the uncertain. It is an act of faith. Step 1 avoids people fearing they lack the *competence to change*. Of course, since the new ways of doing things are unknown, this fear is just a belief.

Change often necessitates changes in skills. Some people will feel that they won't be able to make the transition very well. They don't think they can do it. During the step 1 meetings, they are asked to define action plans that include how to build the new skills if needed. This will be defined with the emotional and social support or encouragement of peers they have learned to trust during the step 1 meetings. They thereby start to believe the can do it.

Step 1 also avoids people being overloaded and overwhelmed. Again, this is just a belief. During the step 1 meetings, the people themselves define the scope and content of the change they have the ability and desire to implement locally. Experience shows that employees have a tendency to be more ambitious and demanding of themselves when they are given the opportunity and power to define what they need to do to succeed than if it is defined by someone else. So the fact that the action plans are defined collectively reduces the risk of over-ambitious changes, which would discourage people to contribute to the

Slim Lambert

change. They therefore start to believe the have the possibility to implement changes.

Step 1 meetings avoid people fearing that current situations cannot be addressed differently. Indeed, using Appreciative Inquiry Methodology as the backbone of the meeting, it changes human mindsets by switching the focus of their attention. This methodology, often confused with positive thinking, focuses on the power of questions to create the energy, knowledge, and images that allow significant transformation of beliefs. Beliefs about how to address the current situation are changed as expectations we hold are changed. Questions are used to make people acknowledge their strengths, aspirations, and opportunities, and then to make them build on them to create a belief in the desired state. You make people focus on what they want more of, not what they want less of—what could be and what works. As people define new solutions to address the theme, they define things they need more of or that they need to do differently. As they look at the history and compare themselves to people different from themselves, they are reminded that whatever you want more of already exists, even if only in small quantities. During the meetings, they also realise that it is easier to create change by amplifying the positive qualities of a group or organisation than by trying to fix the negative qualities. *Then they start believing in the desired states.* Getting people to inquire together into the best examples of what they want more of creates its own momentum. The methodology is based on a deceptively simple premise: organisations and people grow in the direction of what they repeatedly ask questions about and focus their attention on. You do not focus on changing people. Instead, *you invite people to engage in building the kinds of organisations they want to live in.* That's hard to resist. And it is a great way for people to take the (low) risk of starting to believe in the desired state.

Engaging the organisation in positive dialogue to create multiple positive possibilities, moves the organisation and the people in the direction of the desired states. Dialogue and, thus, language is the creator of a desired reality because the language we use creates our reality. The methodology is about creating your own future by establishing self-fulfilling prophesies. It does not mean denying the issues. People discover what makes them and the organisation great and then expand on it. The design of the change, therefore, is focused on strengths. The questions we ask, the things we focus on, the topics that we choose, determine what we find. This is used to build the belief toward the desire states. Leaders enhance this by establishing a frame, which is the theme of the step 1 meeting tool. The seeds are implicit in the very first question the leader asks through the theme.

Slim Lambert

A theme is a question that prompts a solution-focused search for a something that might require change in the way things are done.

Criteria of a powerful theme are:

- it guides toward a change but is not completely indicative of what the change is or how to implement it;
- it prompts a leap in the unknown;
- it guides and steers toward the intuition about the change the leader has;
- it leaves room for flexibility and responsiveness;
- it gives clear direction and, at the same time, is general enough to allow individuals to enhance it along the way of the dialogues and experimentations;
- it focuses on what works well;
- it focuses on the whole, not the parts, of the organisation or the business topic;
- it concentrates on the interfaces and boundaries of components of the organisation and their connections and arrangement;
- it facilitates the creation of alternative scenarios for the future, the first definition of the change, or for the solution it embeds;
- focuses on the question of what is going on now in the organisation in terms of key issues, challenges, concerns, and core questions;

- it opens the way for an area where careful thought and attention can produce profound results;
- it is simple and clear;
- it is thought provoking;
- it channels the inquiry flow it prompts;
- it surfaces assumptions;
- it opens new possibilities;
- it invites exploration;
- it triggers inquiry and discovery rather than advocacy;
- it surfaces new ideas and possibilities;
- it creates forward movement;
- it enables discovery of the organisation's bottlenecks, constraints, and the major issues that hold it back from achieving its purposes;
- it focuses on what you want, not on what you don't want;
- it enables to think about a time when things were working at their very best;
- it is meaningful to the stakeholders and participants who are invited to attend;
- it keeps people away from problem solving and keeps them focused on creating a type of environment that would prevent problems rather than merely trying to remedy existing problems;
- it triggers global exploration of the topic at hand, before exploring local actions;
- it triggers future focus and common ground focus between stakeholders;
- it triggers self-management and responsibility for decisions and actions;

Slim Lambert

- it opens a search into the realm of new possibilities;
- it enables understanding of the current situation;
- it avoids predetermined outcomes or answers;
- it illuminates the most exciting possibilities for the whole;
- it is not focused, at least initially, on finding an immediate answer or a solution;
- it enables to discover the right questions to ask in relation to a critical issue;
- it engages people's values, hopes, and ideals—that is, relates to something that's larger than themselves, to which they can connect and contribute;
- it is not about removing pain or fixing problems, but rather about evoking collective possibilities;
- and it gets people excited and energised.

A powerful theme prompts people to address sub-questions such as:

- What would it take to create change on this issue?
- What could happen that would enable you to feel fully engaged and energised in this situation?
- What is possible here and who cares about it?
- What needs our immediate attention going forward?
- If our success was completely guaranteed, what bold steps might we choose?
- How can we support each other in taking the next steps?
- What unique contribution can we each make?

- What challenges might come our way, and how might we meet them?
- What seed might we plant together today that could make the most difference to the future of our situation?

Examples of themes are:

- How can we retain our best people?
- What would this workplace be like if it were the kind of place I looked forward to getting up and coming to every morning?
- What question if answered could make the greatest difference to the future of situation X?
- How can we become the obvious natural partner for the business units?
- What opportunities can we see in situation X?
- What are the dilemmas and opportunities in situation X?
- How could the organisation be better?
- How can we fix the problems in the business unit?
- What could a good organisation also be?
- Why would it be important and how could we improve profitability, market value, and returns on capital employed?
- What kind of company are we going to be?

2.7.1. Overview—what is it and what are its phases?

It is an off-site meeting lasting for two and a half days. It is planning process that makes possible the development of common ground among groups or organisations with diverse interests regarding the theme. It allows for the development of a shared vision and specific local change action plans.

The process allows for the creation of shared visions and initiates the deployment of those visions by creating self-managing teams responsible for working the specifics of how to make the plan happen globally and locally. It brings a whole system into the room to work on a task-focused agenda.

The process emphasizes collaborative, experiential learning and community planning.

It revolves around four main tasks:

Participants examine the past and present. They are able to reach an understanding of the history of the whole system and how it is shaping the present and the future. This is achieved through the interaction of the participants who identify, evaluate, and adapt to trends in their environment. They are able to envision the future, which is shared by all segments of the organisation, and arrive at individual and stakeholder commitments toward required actions. They acknowledge the full range of realities facing themselves and others. They discover where in the organisation their ideas of the desired state are shared.

Participants then propose a series of alternative scenarios of the future—visions they themselves are willing to make happen. They identify the major issues facing the organisation. They agree on overall purpose for the change.

Participants then choose a shared set of goals and methods from the set of scenarios.
Large, diverse participant groups discover purposes, projects, and values they hold in common. Participants create a desired future together and start action planning right away.

Finally, participants generate and commit to action steps that involve them and the rest of the organisation. They build a strong sense of community. They decide who needs to be involved in the change. They determine what influence the people involved should have. They clarify what information is needed to make decisions. They self-select themselves to action planning teams.

Lets look into more details about what goes on during the meeting. *I will share the actions sheets the facilitator hands out to participants.* They explain to participants what they are asked to do during each exercise. I will also comment some of these to help you adapt them to your context.

Slim Lambert

Have people sit in mixed groups, each a cross-section of the whole meeting participants.

The action sheet to hand out is:
The task here is to focus on the past. The purpose of a history session is to develop a shared knowledge of where the system has come from, and all the major events or changes that it has gone through, so you can all work from the same body of knowledge.

The history session focuses on learning about the organisational system's evolution. It is not about an individual's personal history, although individuals are involved in the history of their organisation.

Review the history of the organisation's major events, milestones, achievements, and tragedies that have shaped the character of the organisation's historical events, turning points, crises, positive deviants and legends that have had a significant influence on the development of their organisation. Identify changes that have been going on out there in the world in the past twenty years that are significant.

Use long strips of butcher paper on the walls, with titles: "Personal," "Global," and "X" (i.e., the theme proposed for this meeting), and date every five or ten years so that twenty years are covered.

Think about memorable personal, global, and local (future search topic) events that represent notable milestones and/or turning points.

Use a marker to write (or draw) your notes on time lines on the wall.

Note milestones you have experienced over twenty to thirty years on the long strips on the wall.

In small groups, talk over the trends and patterns that you see.

Tell us a story and note how it relates to the other time lines. (Get those who have been employed the longest, with the most experience to speak up first, so they can provide a historical perspective.)

As the time line of storytelling approaches the present, consider the best aspects of your history, the things you want to preserve and continue forward.

Focus on:

- things that have happened at the global level over the last twenty to thirty years;
- what has happened to our organisation over the same time span;
- what has happened to us personally during that time;
- the meaning and significance of the trends from the data;

- recent events or emergent trends that may be signs of things to come;
- changes in the world over the last five to seven years that strike you as significant or novel;
- milestones and turning points in the organisation;
- major events or historical developments that were significant in making your organisation what it is today;
- unique things about the history and evolution of your organisation.

The most significant trends will be reported in a plenary session to the community present in the meeting. So prepare public summaries of stories derived from everybody's experiences.

Comments on the process:
This task gets every person in the room writing on flip charts showing that they all have valid information and experience. Moving around is encouraged. All items remain on the walls to the end.

The first task establishes personal histories, key world events, and milestones in the life of "X." This enables participants to share an integrated picture—how each set of events is related to the others.

How far back should you review the past? To organize a review of the past, create three time lines divided into three or four eras. Eras can be related to the age of "X," critical events in the life of "X," and the age of the oldest conference participants. Default eras are the 80s, 90s, until now.

Knowledge of the past usually seems to bring participants closer together. It offers a deeper appreciation for the work of their peers, the challenges they've faced, and the pride people have had working for the organisation over the years. The telling of past events, reminiscing about the details of significant turning points, and their relation to how the organisation has evolved over time brings out the meaning and rich context behind the changes the people will identify later. Participants come to perceive the interdependencies between different trends that are the cause of turbulence and uncertainty that will prompt the need for a change or a new solution. As the list of major events grows longer on the time line, the changing world appears before everyone's eyes.

You pull people together as a community. In a way, the history session restores the oral tradition that once thrived in preliterate cultures in which people shared their common history, customs, and rituals, and paid homage to their ancestors with the spoken word.

The history session reinforces the need for belongingness (the communal sense that this is our place and this is our history). A history session can be compared to a form of learning that mobilizes the collective memory. As the time approaches the present in the history session, more members become involved in contributing to the community story.

In the history session, the community begins to explore the unique character of its system, its distinctive competence, its culture, and its other familiar features. These might be the strengths or levers to build on.

The exercise awakens people to the fact that proactive and planned change is in their best interest and that to survive the wake of turbulence requires creative collaboration and innovative responses. The session thus contributes to openness and begins the process of building trust. As participants add to the list of perceptions and the database grows, they become aware that they are all living in the same world.

The environmental scan of changes in the world can produce a great deal of data easily interpreted in negative terms. The initial reaction can be one of gloom and doom because people are reacting emotionally to the turbulence and the perception of a world spinning out of control.

This exercise helps people to come to terms with the realities of the environment and social forces that are impinging on their system. People begin to recognize that they all had been struggling and fighting for the same cause.

2.7.3. *Exercise No. 2: Explore the present external trends, the stakeholder perspective*

The action sheet to hand out is:
Reorganize into stakeholder groups, people with a shared relationship to "X."

Identify trends important to you. You will report to the whole participants of the meeting what you are doing and what you want to do in the future about these trends.

Review external trends that are shaping your lives and organisation *now*.

Put your group's perceptions of world trends into a "mind map."

A giant map is created on the wall with the "X" in the middle.

You want to map all the external trends that are having an impact on "X" now. Your mind map is compiled as a total group, so everybody needs to hear what matters to others, and take one trend at a time.

This should be an interactive community experience. Ideas and connections trigger other ideas and connections. So when somebody calls out a trend, ask yourselves, "Is that a new issue or does it branch off of something already there?" If new, draw a new line from the centre in a different colour.

As those you speak out connect their issues to those already on the map, draw each cluster of related issues in its own colour.

If people flag opposing trends, put both perceptions up, and always ask for concrete examples.

Group tension might rise and there may be pressure to keep moving. Don't give in to it. You are not seeking time efficiency.

Slim Lambert

Take the time to validate every person's reality. Every person who volunteers an item is worth our time. No contribution, however off-beat or obscure, is irrelevant.

Many people are not used to thinking descriptively. So when you hear solutions instead of trends, ask, "What trend is that a solution to?" If you hear problems, ask what trend that problem reflects.

It is particularly difficult to get people to stay with the impact of external trends on their organisational part. Nearly always, a number of participants are more invested in the impact of trends on them. Accept what you hear, restate that you seek a collective portrait of world and societal trends.

Once you have finished the mind map, each person will use a strip of seven sticky dots, colour-matched by stakeholder group. Each of you is asked to place the dots on the trends they consider most important for the "X." You may put all seven on one trend, four on one and three on another, or on seven different trends, for example. You will probably end with seven to ten priorities, but that is not the purpose of this exercise.

Once this is done, look at how you feel about what you are doing now vis-à-vis "X." Focus on the important trends. This is not aimed at duplicating mind map analyses. Remember, the mind map task is descriptive of what we are doing, what we want to do, and how we feel about what we are doing. It represents current reality.

This "are doing" activity is a bout making lists of "prouds" and "sorrys" with regards to what you are doing in relationship to "X." Ask yourself, What aspects of our current organisation do I want to keep? Drop? Create? Note on your map, or on separate support, what you are doing now and what you want to do that you are not doing now about trends you consider important. Give examples. Speak in terms of who and what.

But, "own it, don't moan it." Hear what others are saying, beyond blaming and complaining. Lists are to be viewed as current reality, not as problems to be solved. The purpose is to depict reality, not finger-pointing.

Comments on the process:
Groups experience each one owning up and taking responsibility. Everybody gets to hear each person's observations and examples of trends each considers important. "My facts" and "your facts" become our facts. One usually does not take the time to recognize how many external forces impinge on us! This recognition is often a low moment in the conference as people wonder, How on earth are we going to make sense of all this?

It is at this point in the conference that the community begins to engage the chaos. Participants recognize that their pet solutions (everyone has them) will not work, they also recognize that they are in this together. They realise they cannot cope alone. Outside forces create pressure for change and push people to organize. It is about owning the complexity and struggling with it that seems to encourage community.

Mind mapping is especially powerful in helping a group make visible a broad pattern of concerns. Collectively we are aware of nearly everything. Mind mapping is not a poll to set priorities but rather visual data for the dialogue that will take place next about the future. You do not wish to reconcile these perceptions through agreement *or* avoidance.

By asking every person where on the map to put his or her item, and what words to use, you avoid interpreting, controlling, or shaping people's thoughts. Moreover, you get richer information as they call out their items, build on each other's connections, and give examples of what they mean.

People often express awe (fear mixed with wonder) at the complexity. Sometimes this takes the form of stunned silence. Sometimes it takes the form of looking for somebody to blame for "distracting us" with so many issues. Sometimes this leads to a rash of positive trends, sometimes to a search for reasons. I believe the strong feelings building up in a group at this point are natural, inevitable, and functional if the meeting is to succeed.

Eventually the exercise winds down with a few people still having items to put in and most of the group fidgeting and ready to quit. That is a very good place to stop.

The stage is set for discussing and accepting responsibility for action. The point of the exercise is not to set priorities. Rather it's a step toward dialogue and manageability. You want participants to acknowledge paradox and confusion. You want to make it harder for people to hold to the fantasy that "we" are clear on the situation and "they" are confused, or vice versa. The truth is that none of us has the truth.

As each group reports the mind map, you hear for the first time the extent to which stakeholders share common or divers concerns. These observations usually go unspoken in ordinary meetings. People are surprised at which groups care about what, and realise that a lot of us worry about the same issues and want to live in the same kind of world.

As each group reports back to the conference on what they are doing now and what they will do in the future, they see how they fit into the bigger picture and at the same time take ownership of their part of the picture.

2.7.4. Exercise No. 3: Ideal Future Scenarios Create Ideal Future Scenarios

Participants now leave their stakeholder groups.

The action sheet to hand out is:
One question you will ask yourself concerns the trends defined by the "prouds" and "sorry" you have identified represent the changes that have taken place. With that thought in mind, what will the probable future be if these changes continue on their present course? One half of the room will concentrate on the most probable future.

Another question you will ask yourself concerns the other side of the coin: the desirable state. What would you like to happen if the best possible things occur instead of the worst? The other half of the room will concentrate on the most desirable future for the world.

Each group is to come up with four to five scenarios and describe them in five or six key statements. Consider these statements to be your strategic goals.

Put yourselves twenty years in the future and present the scenario as if it were happening now. To imagine future scenarios, build on what works. Develop plans and steps to make the vision you have a reality. Look for solutions that already exist. Amplify what is working. You have fifteen minutes per scenario.

Report the group lists in a brief five-minute presentation to the community. Present your scenario any way you choose. I recommend creative presentations—a drama, skit, play, and TV news show, for example. Ensure everybody participates rather than having a single person report for the group.

Then, each group will walk around the meeting room and looks for overlaps with other groups. If two groups agree one overlaps, they write them on the common ground board.

Overlaps are themes or potential projects. The board is divided in two lists: common future themes (what we want or will happen) and potential projects (how to get there).

Comments about the process:

By imagining and then acting out ideal futures, people anchor them in their brains, bodies, and psyches. At this point, people often rise to the heights of aspiration and idealism, the polar opposite of where they were earlier in the meeting.

Behind every drama presented in the scenarios, no matter how fanciful, lies a bedrock of reality, grounded in every person's day-to-day experience. Acting out and sharing our dreams as if we are living them now contributes greatly to widespread implementation.

This task develops a set of strategic goals that will bring about the most desirable future for the organisation toward "X."

The what-will-happen predictions automatically become "what we desire to happen," as participants define what needs to be done. (This is one soft way to bring people with a strong problem-focused mindset into a solution-focused mindset.)

2.7.5.   *Exercise No. 4: Action Planning Makes Action Plans*

The action sheet to hand out is:

Self-selected groups will now make short- and long-range action plans for implementing their ideal desired states.

First, with the groups you were in previously, each of you propose your ideas as to how to reach the common goals expressed by yours or others' groups. You also identify constraints and levers that exist (forces for and forces against). Identify a list of the most serious constraints, together with strategies for dealing with or getting around them. You have less than one hour to complete this task. Place the ideas (written on Post-it Notes) under the appropriate goal.

Second, select the future initiative you want to work on. You now have a chance to "put a stake in the ground" and invite others who have energy for a particular project or theme to join you. You will report to the others before closing, and make plans for disseminating the outcomes. So, take the opportunity to collaborate across boundaries. Each of these groups use the notes posted for their goal as seeds.

Action planning needs to specify the tasks you will accomplish in the next three weeks, three months, and three years. Your plans for action should specify several things: exactly what activities need to occur by a given date, who will be responsible and provide support, what other people not currently in attendance need to be involved in the implementation of your plans, and how you are going to get those people involved in the implementation effort.

Third, you participate in the action planning fair. It works as follows: In preparation for the fair, each action planning group prepares a brief report on a flip chart. The action planning groups break up and reform in mixed groups, each including at least one person from each action planning group. Each of the newly formed mixed groups takes their seats at one of the action planning tables. The representative of the action planning team whose flip chart is at the table provides a brief report and solicits feedback from the rest of the mixed group. (All the groups go through this step at the same time.).

Comments about the process:
Once people decide on their goals and commit to next steps, they are likely to sustain the energy to involve others and stay connected. This is a crucial moment in the meeting because out of the commitment to these common futures springs commitment to action.

Unlike traditional strategic meeting sessions, the meetings tools deal with constraints as close to the end of the meeting as possible. Concentrating on constraints in earlier stages tends to inhibit the growth of confidence and creativity in large groups.

Participants usually select strategic goal areas that involve their expertise and the ones they are committed to implementing. This results is the formation of a number of groups dedicated to working on the development and implementation of detailed action plans on behalf of the whole community. These groups will recruit people to help them implement the action plans. So the groups quickly become communities of action.

The important part of the process is the opportunity for individuals or groups to put a stake in the ground and invite others with energy and commitment around a particular project to join them.

Slim Lambert

What should be done after the meeting to ensure the implementation of action plans?

People invariably create projects and structures that take on a life of their own. These are not consultant-driven, nor do they require a lot of outside help to keep doing. However, this is where the leader helps people take responsibility for making sure that self-selected task forces are supported and that information on progress is shared with the larger community.

The leader sets the environment; it's the people who drive the action. Exercising leadership this way requires no extraordinary skills or concepts. Instead of seeking to coordinate task forces by remote control, you only need somebody capable of finding a space, arranging for refreshments, and sending out a meeting announcement.

Anything works that increases everyone's ongoing view of the whole and that supports people acting on their own. Anything fails that leaves people in the dark about what others are doing and deprives them of initiative. One practice that usually fails is assigning coordination and control of action plans to a person or group not engaged in doing the work.

Examples of follow-up actions to facilitate include:

- a follow-up meeting held three months later to find out what the various groups are doing and to see if additional resources are needed;

- periodic reconnecting for up to a day;
- newsletters;

Creating a flow of news from each to all takes many forms, including email list servers, and newspapers on line and in hard copy.

- Web sites.

These sites can be as simple as a posting of the meeting reports and other documents. They can be as elaborate as ongoing dialogue groups within and between groups.

- a "buddy" system for people who did not attend the meeting;
- the creation of an entity that coordinates action and continuing activities.

It may be either a management responsibility or the work of a continuing, authorized group.

All these follow-up actions need to cover topics such as:

- what we said we were going to do;
- what we have done;
- what we're going to do next;
- what help we need.

3.   STEP 2

3.1.   What are the objectives of this step?

The objective of this step is to inspire and energise thanks to *a vision of the applicable-to-all change of the organisation.*

Defining the vision will *reinforce and help implement the small changes* defined at step 1. It will give them coherence and add elements of change in order to increase the return of investment of these small changes for the global organisation. It will create synergies and alignment. It will help sustain the momentum and the intention for change over time.

Based on the concrete elements gathered, you will build an ambition and direction of the applicable-to-all change initiative. You envision what could be. Lessons learned from step 1 of the REFRESHING change management process serve as data for a feasibility check of the applicable-to-all change. The data generated by the impact analysis, and assessment of the organisation's capacity to take on the small changes provide the basis for making a more realistic decision about the applicable-to-all change initiative's content and time line. You need to keep the human factors in mind for this decision. Too often, we find competent people having emotional breakdowns over unrealistic time pressures they cannot renegotiate.

The vision will *institutionalize and celebrate small changes* and wins that result from implementing step 1 change actions.

If you think about how we traditionally celebrate wins, we wait until the change is over before rewarding employees for the difficult work of change. But by the point that the change is done, most employees are feeling fine and not resisting. The reward becomes a perk instead of a motivator. Thanks to step 2 of the process, we instead apply them during the hardest moments of change. The vision defined in step 2 is a way to recognize and honour those who are implementing local change actions. So step 2 can start shortly after step 1 or before it ends. It can be run parallel to the implementation of the local action plans defined in step 1 meetings. Ideally, however, you should give the time for these actions plans to produce results and offer lessons.

Actually, a lot of changes have already taken place locally and many new solutions to the theme implemented. But the goal is now to *use the vision to generalize these or similar solutions*. However, you do not want a one-size-fits-all solution implemented everywhere. The questions to answer are: How can an applicable-to-all change initiative reinforce and sustain local changes and the core idea shared by all the local change initiatives? How can it encourage those who have not been involved in step 1 to adopt the core idea of the local change initiatives?

A vision is not intended to inhibit initiatives and must never be allowed to do so. It recombines them creatively in a new and successful fashion. You do not slash and burn what exists in order to create the promised land. *You start with what you already have.* You look at existing parts of the organisational solutions for the theme. Indeed, too much "creative destruction" burns out companies. By looking around to see what you already have in place that could be reused to craft the change vision, you define easy-to-implement and cost-efficient solutions. You do not need to obliterate the past to create the future. The smarts of the leaders is not in the fact that they figure out the required vision; it is in the fact that they the vision as a result of recombining existing changes. This can produce a lot of gain with much less pain. The "no pain, no change" cliché is fallacious, or worse, a cynical excuse to justify all forms of badly managed change. Using step 1 to build the vision, avoids repetitive-change syndrome, change weariness, initiative overload, and a corrosive cynicism that builds with each wave of destructive-based change, making each succeeding wave all the more difficult to manage. So the definition of the vision of the change relies on discovering and pulling out the existing organisational assets, redeploying them, and recombining them to reach new ends. It capitalises on lessons learned and previous investments of money and efforts linked to changing. It also avoids the not-invented-here syndrome.

The vision will also *inspire people to achieve remarkable things*. People are stimulated into change by being challenged to achieve something remarkable. Since the vision is based on step 1 actions, you show confidence in people's ability to leave their comfort zone and do what has not been done before. This is most effective when people create their own stretch goals as they have done in step 1. An realistic and desirable vision *paints a picture of a very appealing future.* The vision considers the long-term interests of all stakeholders. If groups of stakeholders believe they are forced to make unreasonable sacrifices, they

Slim Lambert

will not be committed to the vision. This is avoided because the vision is done after step 1, when stakeholders are strongly involved and empowered. One of the secrets of happiness has been found to be an achievable challenge. The vision will be achievable because step 1 has proven that local versions of the change are achievable.

This vision will *pull people not yet involved in step 1* change actions to work on what others might think is impossible. Since it is based on step 1, they have to achieve the vision to remain credible. And when they do, they gain much credibility. This creates a virtuous circle.

A vision is a catalyst for people to embark on activities that cut across the organisation. Change actions at step 1 were local with the global in mind. With the *vision, you drive a global action with the local in mind!* A vision enables efficient goal setting and planning. It helps people set priorities. The vision says, "This is what we stand for." It defines what people should do, as well as what they should not do. It unleashes energy. It is the embodiment of the organisation's core beliefs. It provides focus for assessing individual, department, and organisational progress. It defines the priority domains of change. It identifies the major issues of change. It ensures that everyone is pulling in the same direction, while still allowing individuals room to manoeuvre—for example, to pursue change actions defined in step 1.

The vision is what defines the ultimate objective of change, specifies which parts or elements of the organisation will be affected by it, and establishes the main features of the what and how of change. The vision shows the direction change will take and the goal it is to achieve. It acts as a guiding light amid the chaos of change. Everyone who is affected by change, however slightly, acts with reference to the vision. It provides a framework within which everyone knows how to act and how to tackle unexpected situations by making decisions that are consistent with the purpose of change. It is entirely compatible with the role of managers as leaders, directing and guiding the organisation while empowering people to define and implement changes. It articulates the reasons behind the decision to change. It makes the change meaningful. It defines the extent of change, that is, how profound it will be, how long it will take, and in which domains it will operate. It demonstrates the global reach of the change by stipulating the major issues at stake. It can also lessen the sense of journeying into the unknown (although step 1 actions reduce this anxiety of the unknown).

3.1.1.   *How do you ensure commitment to the vision of the global applicable-to-all change initiative?*

Through the process of defining it and because it's origin is in the step 1 outputs produced by those who need to change, and the stakeholders. So the commitment should and is often a no-brainer.

There is still a selling act to do because not all have been involved and because the vision is something that relates to a global cause or raison d'être. This selling act, however, is one of clarifying or explaining what the change means on a daily basis. The ingredients for commitment to the vision are already present and just need to be capitalised on.

3.1.2. *What characterises a good vision?*

It is a story! It is not a statement. A mission is a statement. A mission statement tells what business you are in and what products and services you will offer. It is a statement of purpose. A mission statement may last for decades.

A vision transforms the organisation. It provides *a picture of what could be.* It is a catalyst that can compel an organisation to move toward a dream. As dreams come true or realities change, visions change. It is a goal of the highest order. It indicates how the organisation will act. Each vision is unique to your organisation.

A vision shows how diverse parts of the organisation are aligned in pursuit of common goals. A vision embraces paradox. As you begin thinking about creating a vision, you will find many issues seem to be either/or in nature. For example, either we go for low cost or we go for high quality, or either we invest for the future or we focus on short-term goals. Good vision statements accept both sides of the paradox. For example, we strive to achieve low costs and guarantee high quality. Managing these seemingly paradoxical issues is what gives life to visions.

So the vision cannot be a simplistic statement. It should be a script of scenarios. It needs to be an illustrative story painting a broad canvas with a picture of tomorrow's organisation. I recommend that the minimum length of the vision be a very full one page!

For a vision to be clear, it must be detailed, richly textured, and written from several perspectives about what it means for people on a day-to-day basis. It should not be just succinct bullet points. There should be complete and illustrative sentences. To be understood, the vision must be presented to employees very much like we would present the contents of a new movie or play to actors. It must be a story in which the people are the "stars." The quality check is that you avoid the reaction, "That's nice, but what does it mean for me, or, what are we supposed to do?" The vision must be *related to the work of people*. This is one reason a truly good vision can only be defined after step 1!

How do you write a good story? This will be detailed in the step "sponsored projects."

3.1.3.   *Who should be involved in defining the vision? What is the process?*

Remember, the vision does not only belong to top management. It will only be an effective force for change if people feel that the vision belongs to them. The power of a vision comes truly into play only when the people themselves have had some part in its creation.

The goal is to *build a story by collecting stories from step 1 actions* and from positive deviants. They will be the ingredients of the vision story.

You want to run several parallel workshops to collect stories, then share these stories in a workshop to build the *draft* of the vision. This workshop should invite a panel of those who have shared stories and of those that have been involved in step 1. It needs to be a selection of the whole organisation. Ideally, it is people nominated by participants of the previous story sharing meetings.

After this workshop you then cascade this draft of vision and enrich it before it is finalized by the leaders.

Below is the agenda of the workshop and some tips.

Step 1. Take stock and build on what you know.

- Create or remind people about the mission statement (optional).

If your organisation does not have a clear mission statement, then you should begin with this activity. The mission statement should address whom the organisation should serve, what they should receive, and the ultimate result you seek. A mission statement should be relatively short—under one hundred words, if possible.

- Hold a conversation that focuses on the questions: Who is the customer for the vision? Who is going to use the vision? How will it be used?
- Restate the original theme addressed in step 1.
- Present the findings of step 1 meeting tools and subsequent implementation of action plans.
- Give meaning by reframing.

To reframe means to change the conceptual or emotional setting or viewpoint in relation to a situation that is experienced and to place it in another frame that fits the "facts," thereby changing its entire meaning. Reframing leaves the facts alone but may well challenge assumptions and filters. Reframing means changing the emphasis locus point. For example, a request for a pay raise may be reframed as an imperative to keep talented people.

Why reframe? For most organisations confronting the need to transform, the temptation to engage in simple extrapolation from current purpose to future purpose is very great. Linear extrapolation from current to future purpose is probably the most common failure.

How do participants do the reframing? Each subgroup in the workshop asks four questions:

1. How can we reformulate what people say, as what it means in terms of root causes, levers, and so on, for the whole organisation?

First, identify the frame of the people who made the changes (i.e., inferences made because of their beliefs, values, assumptions, experience, selected data). This will help answer the following questions: What other causes to the problem are there? What other solutions to the problem are there? What other causes can be served by the solution? How can we look at it another way? For example, a problem as an opportunity; a weakness as a strength; an impossibility as a distant possibility; a distant possibility as a near possibility; oppression (against me) as neutral (doesn't care about me), unkindness as lack of understanding.

This quality check will then enable to answer the question what needs to be changed?

Second, ask, What worked well in each story, what were the solutions adopted? How can we translate the story into capabilities of the organisation? What could be the useful recombination of existing solutions (e.g., re-use, re-deploy, re-combine, mimic, etc.)? What can be reused to craft the changes you need? How can we translate: interpret, reinvent, and render existing solutions useful in a different situation? How can we, with a little customization and translation, adapt these solutions to the need we have?

Summarize and list all solutions to addressing the theme that stand out as feasible and impactful. Select the top five.

Step 2. Create a vision statement.
First, make people visualize. Ask them to sit quietly and relax. Don't rush this visualization process. People need time to settle in and explore images. Say, "For the next couple of minutes just sit quietly. Don't write anything; just relax. Imagine the future—three to five years from now. Imagine your organisation has become everything you've hoped for thanks to these top five solutions. Explore this image.... Who is in it?... What's going on in the scene?... What makes it so ideal?... What are people saying?... What are they doing?... Now, let that image go.... Allow another image to come into view. ... Explore this image.... Who's in it?... What's going on?... Where are you in this scene?... What's it feel like to work here?... Now, allow this image to fade."

Second, put it in a format of elevator speech.

Slim Lambert

"For the next three minutes, jot down what you envisioned during this exercise. Please don't talk during this exercise." Allow time for writing. "Please sit quietly again and close your eyes. Imagine that time in the future again. A reporter from *The Wall Street Journal* is going to do a story on your organisation. What would you show the reporter as examples of things that make you particularly proud? Be specific in your thinking and explore this image in some detail. Take a couple of minutes to jot down the images that came to mind during this last visualization exercise."

Third, make them discuss it.

Pairs talk about what they envisioned. A talks for ten to fifteen minutes. B finds out everything they can about what A envisioned. Switch roles. It is important to keep the attention on the speaker. When A is talking, B should be in listening mode—asking questions, clarifying, and so on. B should not be giving his or her thoughts during this round. When you switch, A should follow the same guidelines. Give each pair ten index cards or large Post-It Notes. Ask them to pick ten items to put forward in the whole group.

Fourth, do a plenary session.

With the full group, ask for one card from one pair. Post it. Ask for one card from another group. Post it. Continue this process until all the cards are posted. Begin grouping the cards as you post them.

Step 3. Formalise the vision.

Have the subgroups answer the questions below.

Why change? What is the ideal outcome for your change? Beyond creating greater profitability, what is your purpose in making this change? What difference will it make in the lives of your customers? What difference will it make in the lives of the people in the organisation? How will it add value to each of the stakeholders of the organisation? How will this transformation help the organisation better meet the demands of its marketplace? What excites you the most about making this change? What would happen if the organisation did not complete this change successfully? What would be lost? How would the organisation ideally operate to achieve this reality? What will the organisation look like once the change is complete? What will employees say about the organisation once the change is complete? What will customers say about the changed organisation? How will we measure organisational and individual performance in the future?

What to change? Which processes need streamlining? What aspects of operations are outdated? What new market opportunities can be tapped? What processes, structures, goals, and standards will change? How will the company know if this change has been successful? When will key changes occur? What key roles will have to be adapted to support the objectives of the change? What do we have to do in order to be successful— to deliver better value to customers and consumers in the future? What needs to change in order to make that happen? Where do we begin? Which of these changes should we work on first?

What does the change mean in terms of goal setting, reward, recognition, career planning, skills development and training—would all have to be overhauled?

What will not change?

Why change now?

How should we change? What practical and specific solutions demonstrate how to reach targets of the change? What medium- and long-term objectives will be necessary to set subsidiary or intermediate goals? What shorter-term objectives are vital to mobilise the workforce and deliver change? It is important that the objective adopted is in fact the real business objective and not simply a means of achieving it, so where are the leverage points for creating change? Where in the organisation will change offer the greatest opportunity for creating a new operating environment? What intervention-specific actions that interrupt the normal flow of business offer the greatest potential for changing the culture and people's behaviour? Where and when should leaders introduce specific interventions? What are the tactical choices available to change leaders? How could you spell out all the critical changes in a series of from-to messages? How could you make it clear how they will be sequenced and how they will relate to one another?

What is the impact on people? Who will be involved in driving and in what capacity? How will the change affect the way employees currently work? What impact will this have on them? (Will I keep my job? How will pay and benefits be affected? How will this affect my opportunities for advancement?

Will I have a new boss? What new skills will I need? What will be expected of me? How will I be trained and supported for the new challenges? How will my performance be measured? What are the rewards or consequences? What do people need to do both during and after the change? What do you expect from you? How they can contribute to the change?)

Step 4. The final statement.
Ask someone who is a good writer to collect all the comments and write a first draft statement. Do not attempt to write the vision statement in the full group.

Step 5. Infer decision-making criteria.
What makes something important, urgent—for the whole, for our customers, for our stakeholders?

For each of the above, differentiate between "it enables..." and "it avoids...."

Step 5. Infer key behaviours.
These behaviours are the core of what is key in order for all people to contribute actively to the execution of strategic and day-to-day vision of the change. They set the standard about excellence and do's and don'ts of what is expected of people to deliver the change. They provide a compass and criteria for employee's decision-making, for the management of dilemmas (e.g., the choice between time, cost and quality) and for situations not (yet) covered by a process. They communicate what is fair to expect from employees in the context of the new solutions created by the change.

Role modelling leaders must engage in their own development as a core part of the change.

If the change effort is truly to be a success, you must address whether the leaders' mindsets, style, and behaviour favour the future requirements of the organisation. I cannot underscore the importance of this task enough! I can't overemphasize the importance of the leader's personal behaviour in shaping the operating environment. Role modelling is especially key when making decision or behaving in situations *where the stakes are high*, such as when they relate to money, power, recognition, and the building of foundations for the future. And they have to walk the talk when it's very visible even on things that could be perceived as minor to the leader.

People expect a leader, after a period of questioning and soul searching, to decide on a course of action and commit to it without the slightest reservation. They look for leaders to express their personal support, demonstrate confidence in the organisation's ability to reach its goals, and empathize with people during the difficult times. There are tons of things a leader can do. Let's focus on a couple of them.

3.3.1.   *Action number 1: Put a large spotlight on an organisation's leadership team by magnifying their values and behaviours.*

Leaders are on stage in a literal sense during the step 1 meeting tool and figuratively over time in the organisation. Even people who deeply want to believe that things can be different will watch for any crack in the leadership team's commitment or alignment with the new way of doing business, to ensure they do not get fooled into supporting a superficial change process.

How questions are answered, and even what leaders do during breaks in the meetings of the change process are scrutinized. During times of change, these minor issues become symbolic acts to which people attach great meaning. A strong, aligned leadership team that sends messages consistent with new ways of doing business becomes a model of collaboration and commitment to common change goals for the entire organisation. Leaders need to model the change process and the change.

3.3.2. *Action number 2: Ensure recognition during the whole change process.*

People's impression of being part of a success is reinforced when they are shown appreciation of their performance by their peers, superiors, and the leadership team. It is a responsibility of the leader and the line managers to recognise achievements and contributions of people—or preferably of groups—and to see that they are acknowledged. They must identify those people doing well and make it known.

Recognition can take the form of congratulating them verbally or in writing, mentioning them in an in-house journal, or giving a bonus.

In the context of the change process, the leader needs to ensure that line managers are especially attentive to showing recognition to those who deserve it, otherwise the impetus for involvement and commitment that has been created will be destroyed.

What kinds of rewards or recognitions might be helpful during a long change process?

You can find example rewards in the book *1001 Ways to Reward Employees*, which gives many ideas and illustrates ways to offer low-cost incentives. There are hundreds of little ways to tell how much you care about the people in the organisation. Too often, managers think they're showing that they care by giving people patronizing pats on the head. These may take the form of goodies such as gifts, parties, long-service trinkets, trivial newsletters, or "royal visits" (occasional "touring of the troops" with much bowing and scraping)—not that these things are necessarily bad. Like anything, they are neither bad nor good in themselves, but it's in how they're used. When they substitute for treating people as respected and highly valuable partners, they increase cynicism and widen the gap between management and people on the front lines.

Disincentives, penalizing employees who fail to change, are used less frequently. But during periods of change, the true test for people is how much leaders are willing to invest to penalize those who do not change.

What about extrinsic and intrinsic rewards?

Money is the most expensive way to motivate people. Trying to link the objectives of change programs to the compensation of staff rarely enhances their motivation for change. It is exceedingly difficult to incorporate a meaningful link to the change program within compensation systems that are based on a vast array of metrics.

When you think about rewards, do not forget that many studies have found that for human beings, satisfaction equals perception minus expectation. When people do not get the reward they hoped for, they feel punished. The more desirable the reward the more demoralizing it is to miss out. The beauty of this equation for change managers is also that small, unexpected rewards can have disproportionate effects on employees' satisfaction with a change program, compared to expensive and complex monetary rewards.

The pitfalls of monetary and extrinsic rewards are numerous. Threats and coercion destroy motivation and so do rewards. "Do this and you will get that" is not much different from "Do this, or else here is what will happen to you." Moreover, rewards tend to promote blindly a single solution and deter risk-taking. You do not want that during a change process! If people focus on getting a reward, they tend to feel their work is no longer freely chosen and directed by them (if they have to bribe me to do it, it must be something I don't want to do!). You don't want that either during a change process.

It is usually easier to set up or arrange extrinsically motivating conditions than to increase one's intrinsic interest and satisfaction in some behaviour. Experience demonstrates that rewarding someone for carrying out tasks of low interest tends to increase the intrinsic pleasure of doing the task.

Receiving verbal praise and positive feedback increases the intrinsic satisfaction derived from an activity. This is true for both high-interest or low-interest tasks. Make the task like work for pay, or like a job you are directed to do in exchange of a reward, and people will lose some interest. Likewise, rewarding each unit successfully completed or solved (piece work) also reduces intrinsic interest, while often increasing productivity.

On the other hand, when rewards such as praise are based on performance standards that imply one is doing well and performing competently, then the intrinsic interest increases. People like to be told they are doing well.

When designing a reward plan ask yourself questions such as: Is the outcome (reward) of value to them? If it is of value, is it of sufficient worth to change their behaviour? Does the person expect to benefit from a reward if they perform as required? Does the person expect to perform to the standard required if they expend the effort? The important point here is that the level of a person's drive to change their behaviour is not determined by the objectively calculated probabilities that the effort will lead to performance and that the performance will lead to the reward. It is determined by the person's belief about these probabilities.

Also keep in mind that people make judgments about the equity of distributed rewards. If a person considers that the ratio of their work inputs versus the reward outcome is different from other similar people, they will adjust their beliefs or behaviour to bring the perceived imbalance back into line. Remember we are talking about subjective perceptions here!

What remains true is that you should, at each step of the change process, provide people with a pleasurable reward at frequent intervals if they stick to a change. A reward should be given at a pre-defined time. Employees should be informed of this time frame. The positive effect of reward lasts only for a period, research shows—after a while, people want more or take the reward for granted. But after that, the change is to be considered as something normal and is not rewarded.

Of course, whatever the organisation does, it should be careful never to reward anybody, and I mean anybody, for something related to your old, bad behaviour! As an analogy, don't reward a successful week of dieting with a slice of chocolate cake. Reward good dietary behaviour with a manicure or the book you've been wanting.

Finally, do not reward the end result the change seeks to reach. Indeed, they could be reached by sacrificing key behaviours, values, or other results. The trick is to reward the steps toward reaching the sought after results.

3.3.3.   *Action number 3: Send such clear signals as to the treatment of key employees.*

Employees keep close tabs on who is up and who is down, who is in and who is out. Whenever possible, it's important to recognize and reward publicly those who exemplify the attributes called for by the change.

By the same token, it's just as important to impose sanctions on influential key employees who visibly resist or ignore the changes. People need to be given ample opportunity to weigh the new evidence, change their minds, and get on board. But in some cases that just isn't going to happen. Don't demote dissidents and leave them somewhere in the organisation where they can become martyrs for the opposition. If they have to go, then get them out. The removal of even one senior person who is resisting change is a powerful symbolic message that change is real and that resistance to it is a career-limiting move. If the individual in question is acting in ways that clearly violate values important to the new organisation, then the leader has no choice but to act. Lack of action also sends a strong message. In many cases, it makes sense to provide the executive in question with serious coaching and the chance to demonstrate substantive progress within a specified time. If he or she succeeds, terrific; if not, and if the transgressions are sufficiently central to the kind of change you're trying to create, then you have no choice but to get that executive out. But let's be honest, you need to give the person a truly fair assessment before coming to the conclusion he just will not align to the change.

3.3.4. *Action number 4: Symbolic acts*

Symbolic acts can play an important role in generating momentum, energy, and a sense that a new era has begun and there is no turning back. Symbolic acts can be anything from a leader's personal gestures to sweeping decisions. This would include acts such as how money is spent, time is used, with whom you eat, the way you travel, the way you dress, with whom you talk, the size of your office, the way meetings are begin or end, with whom you are seen in videos, and so on. The act has to catch people's attention and illustrate that when things get tough, the leaders are role models.

3.3.5. *Action number 5: Develop a retention strategy.*

An essential objective of any change is to ensure key people remain after the change. Turnover rates often increase dramatically during change with many high performers leaving, either to escape uncomfortable circumstances or through competitor poaching, or because, like everyone else, they are concerned about the future of their job with the organisation. The strategy to address this risk is a key symbolic act.

3.3.6. *Action number 6: Train managers about change management.*

Don't assume that being a great manager is the same as being a great *change* manager. It is your responsibility to help build this key competency among managers and supervisors. The objective is to help them build the skills to be great leaders of change.

Skills to develop are how to:

- generate employee participation and be responsible for driving the change;

- know the skills and goals of each employee and how to gain commitment and involvement to the change;
- deliver the meeting tools of the REFRESHING change management process;
- evaluate where their team members are in the change process (their emotional health) and how to support them through each stage;
- handle the transitions for themselves and their staff;
- understand the current state of the company and the desired state; (This is important in laying the groundwork for questions from employees affected by the change.)
- deal with differences of opinion, to prevent polarization of opinions on one extreme, or "group think" (homogenization of opinions) on the other;
- confront people's inconsistencies between their messages and their behaviour;
- use support tools such as training, external consultants, training, etc.;
- communicate with direct reports about the change;
- demonstrate support for the change;
- identify and manage resistance;
- use basic communication techniques;
- deal with negative employee responses;
- address key talking points, frequently asked questions, and anticipated employee concerns;

3.4.   WHAT ARE THE OBJECTIVES OF THE STEP WORK UNIT BASED
        DIALOGUE WORKSHOPS?

The objective of this step is to let go of any hesitancy to adopt the vision of the change and to let go of the old ways of doing. This is done through workshops that take place inside work units, teams, or departments.

What are the kick-off themes or topics of the dialogue workshops? They can be the vision of the change, the subsequent key behaviours, or urgency and importance criteria. They can be actions taken in step 1. They can be a proposal made by an individual or a manager about how to contribute actively to the vision of the change. They can be on any topic of mutual interest linked to the change.

They are ideally formulated into questions.

3.4.1.   *Why do you need a step focused only on letting go?*

Until people let go of the reality in which they are living, they will not be able to embrace something new. No amount of pleading, selling, or coercion will force them to let go. *You need to let people have enough time to digest the old ways and the change vision.* It is a matter of respect—but not only.

It is also good practice, as explained in the sorrow curve. It is essential to provide the time and opportunity for people to disengage from the current or old state. If these two things are not done, people will go back and forth between the phase of the sorrow curve, and not truly implement the change in an accountable manner.

It is equally important to give people the opportunity to mourn and let go a situation they loved, were used to, that served their interest, and so on. They need to have the chance to say goodbye without guilt, remorse, or repressed grief. From that point forward, they will probably never talk of the past as the good old days but rather as something that is not relevant anymore in the new context.

You want to ensure that all *move out from the contemplation stage.* Sharing the vision and getting people committed to it is not enough. They need a method they can implement in an accountable manner. People stay in the contemplation phase just long enough to create the momentum needed to move on to the next stage, preparation, but not a second longer! You want to pull people spontaneously and honestly to say to themselves something like, "I'll get rid of the things that used to work or habits that do not best serve my interest anymore." It is an opportunity to accelerate voluntary commitment to new behaviours and action plans to align daily actions. It is an opportunity to accelerate the fact that people pursue the search for solutions to contribute to the change actively.

Indeed, analysis paralysis is one of the most dangerous points on the path to creating lasting change. After the vision has been shared, people are faced with a situation where several possible options seem equally valid. They are committed to changing, but they will have a hard time deciding what to do in the present moment. The contemplation stage of change is the point at which an individual or organisation intends to change within a relatively short time horizon, such as within the next six months. In the contemplation stage of change, they are able to see the pros and cons of change as more equal. They may even see change as more positive, but not know how they are going to get there. The reaction can be to engage in ambivalent thinking and doing a lot of planning to plan doing plans of plans of plans to be made. There are studies after studies that produce conflicting results and create so much data that it is impossible to decide on a course of action. The greatest risk at this stage is procrastination. People feel they "should" make a change, but they don't really know how to. But lets not get simplistic. There is also helpful procrastination—it can genuinely help you investigate a change, and it can show you what the change means for you as an individual in your specific context.

Work-unit or team-based dialogue workshops enable you to create the desire to change and a feeling ability to change. People imagine themselves completing it successfully. It reduces fears of any sort linked to the vision of the change, such as fear of the unknown, fear of failure, fear of success.

If people let go, or are assisted in doing so, you see the flip side of anxiety, which is inherent to changing. People not only see new opportunities for the organisation, but also feel personally challenged. They see new prospects for growth and advancement. They feel good about being part of a changing organisation. That kind of enthusiasm is contagious and can be leveraged during dialogue workshops.

3.4.2.   *What happens during dialogue workshops?*

Many of us still live with the idea that "talk is cheap," that most people are "all talk and no action," and that we should "stop talking and get to work." That is often a defensive reaction to something we are not used at doing: having true dialogue, which changes mindset.

Conversations are the way people discover what they know, share it with their colleagues, and in the process create new knowledge for the organisation. In the new economy, conversations are the most important form of work. Conversation is how things get done.

Dialogue sessions are conversations that generate what we call "actionable knowledge." It ensures a cycle of reflection, insight, harvesting, action planning, implementation, and feedback. Conversation is the core process in every step.

During the dialogue workshop, several things happen. People carry not only their own but also others' key ideas into rounds of conversation. This will unfreeze fixed positions and create a more open and exploratory climate for the emergence of new insight.

People build on one another's ideas—everyone contributes from their own perspective to create new understanding. As people make new connections, sparks of insight begin to emerge that no one would have alone. As people move in the rounds of conversation, each person orients to the question of how to contribute to the vision of the change in a different way. It enables them to understand the need or benefit of the act of changing.

The dialogue workshop enables you to build agreement for actions, team-based and individual, for change. It enables groups to decide on a shared commitment for some future state resulting from the change vision. It enables you to design a team-based and individual action plan to implement the change vision. People are empowered to discover what the change means for them on a daily basis in the context of their tribe. It will energise and encourage each person to start planning for action, with the support of his or her tribe. People break the change into small pieces. It creates the opportunity to choose a small task to give a quick and successful contribution to the change.

The dialogue workshop is an opportunity for them to benefit from true dialogue. This enables them to discover and tell their truth to each other about how to implement the change vision. People reflect on their own feelings and thoughts, including their hopes and fears, and listen deeply to one another. People uncover and help resolve what previously blocked their alignment to the change vision.

Slim Lambert

Dialogue workshops are a tool for people managers to launch their support for individual transitions.

3.4.3. *What is the cascading process of the dialogue workshops?*

The process is based on the principle of cascading top-down through the flow of hierarchical teams. It can also be done for a workflow, a transversal process, or a regrouping of roles. The cascade should continue down all relevant levels of the organisation until all teams have done a workshop. In areas with large staffs, it may be necessary for managers to brief their deputies within these teams and ask them to continue the cascading process. In these cases, deputies should be given a brief by their manager. Stakeholders can participate in the workshops, although this is not mandatory. I recommend that one facilitator be responsible for a maximum of twenty-four participants.

3.4.4. *Why do the cascading according to work units?*

First, the required letting go work should be done among people who work together on a daily basis. You want it to concern things that correspond to daily concrete activities and habits of the informal ways of working.

Second, you want people to decide what they will let go. You do not want to make plans for others, and peer pressure is key to this.

Third, you need to do it in small groups because conversation in small groups is our human way of creating, sustaining and changing—or transforming—the realities in which we live.

Below are descriptions of three workshop you could cascade. Depending of the change, the work unit managers can chose to use one or all of them.

It's sometimes called the "if only we knew what we know café." The intention is for people to learn from each other and come to understand each other's differing perspectives. It's not about making decisions—and certainly not about winning arguments.

The objectives of a knowledge café, for each participant are:

- to gain mutual understanding of how each one can and/or will contribute to the change;
- to gain a deeper understanding of other people's perspectives about the change;
- to gain a deeper understanding of one's own views and thinking process about the change;
- to bring to the surface, issues which need airing and exploring about the change;
- to help build a common ground about the change;
- to gain new perspectives about the change;
- to deepen relationships and mutual ownership of the change in the group;
- to enrich one's level of understanding of the change;
- to enhance the understanding of the knowledge or point of view that they and the other participants have;
- and to tease out people's assumptions and insights, as they hear themselves say things.

You will need approximately ninety minutes to run a knowledge café. The number of people should be at least fifteen, though it works best with about thirty. But it can be run with as few as five people and as many as 150.

3.5.1. *Principles that form the basis for a café*

Most of the time is spent in conversation; it is not about one person presenting to the group. The facilitator should not take the lead in the discussions but should listen for problems and remind people gently of the rules of dialogue. The group should be doing the work with minimal intervention from the facilitator. The facilitator can encourage participation and ensure that no one person or group dominates the discussion.

3.5.2. *A facilitator guide and a description of the steps for a café*

The meeting's facilitator introduces its theme and explains how the process will work.

"Four to five people sit at a table and hold a series of conversational rounds lasting from twenty to forty-five minutes about one or more issues or questions that are personally meaningful to them with regards to the theme of the café.

"Each participant is free to:

- state their way of seeing things, their experience, and so on, and ask for feedback from the other participants at their table

Slim Lambert

- or ask a question to the other participants at their table.

"A symbolic 'talking-stick' ensures only the person holding the stick speaks, thus avoiding the discussion becoming dominated by one or a few speakers. No individual speaks for longer than one minute. For that one minute, he or she cannot be interrupted. No one can speak again until everyone has spoken once.

"In round one, you are asked to come up with an overarching question, which, if answered, could make a difference to the question or theme under consideration. It should be constructed as an open question with more than a yes/no or multiple choice answer. To find these questions, ask yourself what core question, if explored, could make the most difference to the situation we're considering? Or what do we not know, that if we did know, could transform this situation for the better?

"That question can be written on a large piece of paper and is the core question for the next two or three rounds of café dialogue at that table. Then one host stays throughout all rounds as the steward for his or her particular table question. At the end of round one, the other people travel to new tables, choosing tables with a new question that interests them. In each round, you write personal insights and thoughts about your table's question on large individual sticky notes that you keep with you as they move to subsequent rounds. The table host or question steward continues to make notes or drawings related to that table's question on the café tablecloth. The host who remained at the table will share the essence of their conversations from the notes and drawings on their tablecloths, and travellers will link and connect ideas they were bringing from their own previous table conversations. Use the following three statements as your dialogue unfolds: 'What I heard you say that I appreciated is...' 'What I heard that challenged my thinking is...' 'To better understand your perspective I'd like to ask you ...'

"The first three rounds take twenty minutes each. Before moving on, take some time to reflect during your inquiry together by asking, 'What is at the centre of our conversation?' "

After three rounds, the facilitator asks the group to wrap up their conversations and gather around a large rolled-out piece of mural paper placed on the rug in the middle of room wall. It looks, in fact, like a large café tablecloth spread on the wall. Each small group is invited to put their individual tablecloths around the edges of the larger cloth and then take a "tour" to notice patterns, themes, and insights that are emerging in their midst. People write one phrase or sentence per sheet that reflects what people were saying publicly during meetings in their unit.

On one paper board people answer the question, What questions should we ask you in order to understand what all this is telling us about your organisation? People are invited to share not only their findings but also their feelings—what the conversation had meant to them personally. People share the patterns, themes, and deeper questions that were emerging from their mutual listening and from the cross-pollination of new ideas being shared.

Last round. People return to their original tables and begin to share the common themes and insights that have emerged from their multiple conversations. If a "guest" senior manager is present at the meeting, a Q&A session can be organized at this stage—he or she can be asked to react to the above mentioned summaries. However, it is important that until this Q&A, the senior manager will have been acting as a "regular" participant and been the "host" of one of the tables.

End the meeting with a peer-to-peer discussion. People find a partner and just walk around the room talking about what they learned that day, or what idea had the most life for them. Then, they link up with two other participants and then the four focus on the deeper themes. They put on a wall paper the essence of what's been explored, what people learned, and possible action steps (or whatever they want as output).

After they have each created their own exhibition, people can take a tour of the other contributions in the gallery—they can also add their insights and put actual comments on each other's contributions. It's like growing a living picture of the whole.

3.6.1.   Overview

The open space approach is largely known for its lack of formal structure. People go wherever they like and participate in whatever topics they find interesting.

The first step is to set the stage by announcing the theme of the meeting. Then small groups convene to address any topic they deem as critical to the theme of the meeting. This is done after people have created the agenda. The agenda is based on what participants have described a topic called a "nightmare" of the theme that they are interested in discussing. So in open space meetings, participants propose topics called nightmares related to the theme of the meeting that will become basis for discussion groups around which participants self-select. The participants create and manage their own set of parallel working sessions around the central theme.

Finally, action planning groups convene around the final grouping of issues. It involves collecting and disseminating the ideas from each meeting. The conveners of each discussion group are responsible for producing a one-page meeting summary, which is posted on a second bulletin board known as "the newsroom." Participants are encouraged to visit the newsroom often. From this point, there are divergent approaches. The strategic plan crafters are determined, or meeting attendees develop strategic plans in groups, or data from the sessions is turned over to senior management for strategic plan crafting (a more traditional approach).

Open space is best suited to situations in which a diverse group of people must grapple with complex and potentially conflicting issues inside the theme of the meeting. Often the solutions identified are innovative, or based on customizing the lessons learned from other people's experiments. The most tangible output from an open space meeting is a set of action points or solutions to explore, for each person taking part in the meeting.

3.6.2.   A facilitator's guide and a description of the steps of an open space meeting

Introducing the exercise

The facilitator starts by presenting: "The one law that forms the basis of an open space meeting is that during an open space event, the law of mobility prevails. You are responsible for your own learning, and this requires you to move to a different discussion group when you are neither learning nor contributing. Rather than remain in a situation in which time is being wasted, you are encouraged to move to a group that meets your needs. All too often, we sit politely in situations that aren't working for us, becoming bored or irritated. It is better to get up and find a situation that works. This partially explains why so much dialogue and learning occurs during coffee breaks at typical conferences. So let's consider the meeting we are going to engage in as an organized break."

The facilitator asks all participants to sit in a half circle, with four to five paper-boards positioned at the corners of the meeting room. If there are more than fifty participants to the meeting, there will probably be several meeting rooms; so in this case, the introduction step can be done in one of these meeting rooms. The facilitator explains the origins of open space technique and how it started:

"In 1997, Harrison Owen, trainer, asked, when did you learn most? The answer was, during the breaks, because of: knowledge of 'my' constraints, free choice of subject, freedom to move around, personal issues or themes, exchange of informal experiences and tips; questions that asked for no one-fits-all solution; no formality; and concrete and immediate Return On Investment. Additionally, he found that almost everything important inside tribes happened in a circle. All important tribal issues were dealt with in open discussion held in a circle. Harrison recognized that there is power and magic in a circle."

Defining the theme of the meeting

The facilitator explains that the objective: "Work on and benefit from the combined experience of X number of participants, which is probably X times the trainer's experience! We will frame the scope of the issues you will have the opportunity to resolve. The theme or a couple of issues that you will have the opportunity to focus on are...."

The facilitator says, "You will have the opportunity to benefit from X number of participants helping you resolve your nightmare. A nightmare is something unpleasant that creeps into all your dreams—something that wakes you up at three in the morning—something that you cannot get out of your head. Think of three nightmares and write them down on the Post-It I am giving you."

Drawing up the meeting agenda
If there are less than twenty participants:

Each participant reads his or her three nightmares. The facilitator reformulates the nightmare into "How can I...?" Then the facilitator asks the other participants if they perfectly understand the issue, and why it is a nightmare. If one of these is similar to one read by another participant, the participant does not read it, but states with whom he or she shares a similar nightmare.

Selection of a few nightmares and creation of the agenda. The facilitator asks who wants to have their nightmare resolved.

Ideally, four nightmares are to be resolved by a group of twelve. If there are less than two volunteers, the facilitator says that it's okay, that anybody can decide to get his or her nightmare solved later on, and that "I suggest that we take the opportunity to postpone the choice after I have explained how the nightmare will be resolved."

If there are more than twenty participants, the facilitator invites fifteen of the selected randomly, to share their nightmares. Then the facilitator invites some of these and other participants to come to the front write the title of the topic, their name, and a timeslot on a sheet of A4 paper. They announce this to the room. Participants can then ask questions about the session and then put their name in the dedicated slot if they are interested in the corresponding nightmare. Participants offering sessions on similar topics may decide to join forces, and people may ask for sessions to be rescheduled to enable them to take part.

This goes on for about fifteen to thirty minutes and soon you have a full schedule.

Whatever the number of participants, the following steps are:

Explanation of how the nightmares will be resolved
The facilitator says:

"Those of you who will be lucky enough to have your issues or nightmare solved will be called clients or flowers (facilitator to decide depending on the audience). The others are going to be called contributors, coaches, bees, or butterflies (facilitator to decide depending on the audience). The role of the contributors is to help the client find his own solution. They should not give the solution because if it's a nightmare, then we should assume that there is no obvious solution. At best, they should explain what they have done in similar situations and how that could be adapted to the client's situation. The best way to achieve this is to act as coach by asking questions to make the client see the situation differently or identify the lever, the true problem, and so on.

Examples of a sequence of questions are: "Tell me (more) about..."; "So what you are saying is..."; "What do you mean by..."; "What leads you to say..."; "What specifically..."; "Can you give me an example..."; "How many...?"

Contributors must follow only one rule: "You have two feet, you must use them, so either you stand by a client or walk around looking for a client to help. (If bees/butterflies, say that butterflies fly around from one flower to the other, whereas bees stay at one flower.) As a facilitator, I have been given the permission to push you around if you stand without doing anything."

The role of clients is to explain the nightmare; receive ideas, suggestions, questions, interpretations; thank the contributors; answer all questions asked; summarize what has been said when a new contributor comes around; and listen and never reject an idea/question.

Kick-off (in each meeting room if there are several)
The facilitator announces that the duration of the open space exercise is thirty minutes per meeting room, but this will be reviewed depending on the way the meetings are run. As an indication, it's enough to allocate at least twenty to thirty minutes to run the exercise, with approximately six nightmares to solve (experience shows that after thirty minutes the participants want to pursue dialoguing).

For gatherings of more than two hundred participants, the facilitator organizes the opportunity for several rounds of open space exercises in order to give the opportunity to all participants to participate to as many sessions/nightmare resolutions as possible.

The facilitator takes away any chairs or things that can serve as blockers of the "you have two feet" rule. The facilitator says, "During the rest of the exercise, I have no role; this is *your* safe space of freedom and creativity. Of course, if you need or want me to contribute as a contributor I would be happy to do so—if you want me to."

Summary
Someone in each meeting room volunteers to make notes and prepares a handwritten or computer-generated report, which is displayed under a sign saying "Session Reports." The whole group reconvenes at certain points, and then at the end of the forum to make announcements and share information.

Action planning
Each participant recollects things he or she has learned or found useful then designs an individual or collective action plan.

3.7.1.   Overview

This workshop empowers each participant to identify which day-to-day behaviours to adopt to be aligned to the key behaviours defined in the vision of the change. The workshop explains what the key behaviours mean for each one. It is a process to launch corrective or improvement actions based on what people say and suggest about how to implement the key behaviours in their day-to-day activities.

The key behaviours workshop is carried out in three to four hours, depending on group size and the level of discussion and interactions.

What are the deliverables?

- An action plan for each individual and for the team to adopt the key behaviours.
- A dialogue enabling feedback to the team leader by team members about the impact of the key behaviours on day-to-day topics.
- A solution finding and action planning meeting.

Participants are in teams of four-to-six people, each team sitting around one key behaviours workshop poster. This is the optimum number to generate a good discussion and to ensure that all participants are fully involved.

The workshop is participant led rather than instructor led. Participants are actively engaged and allowed to discover things for themselves. Being participant led does not mean that as a facilitator you abdicate responsibility. Rather it means that you:

- Convey confidence and enthusiasm for where the change is headed and the achievement of its vision.
- Reinforce the process of the key behaviours workshop throughout the workshop.

Participants are not asked to complete a set of tasks. They are given the opportunity to understand and discuss some of the key issues in organisation and the challenges for the future. People may ask you if their ideas and answers are "right." Take care not to give judgments about these answers. Participants are here to discuss and learn, not to be told.

- Create a safe environment and a sense of trust to promote open discussion.

Promote discussion and dialogue between group members and among team members. Encourage people to be creative in these discussions. Create a dialogue not a debate. Don't let team members get caught up in pointless confrontational games. In a debate, the point is for one side to win. In a dialogue, the point is to clarify what the assumptions, issues, and evidences are. Ensure that there is a balance of voices in the room, so that the discussion is not overpowered by a few strong voices.

- Ensure everyone participates fully.

To do so, you can ask questions to involve quieter participants and manage the more outspoken ones. It is important to openly recognise and value each participant's input. Discourage people from making judgements (such as "we have done this before") or dismissing others' ideas and possibilities for the future.

- Keep people focused on where the change is headed and what they can do to contribute.

Discourages people from lengthy discussions about things they cannot influence. If necessary, arrange to discuss a particular issue with the individual(s) concerned after the workshop.

- Your role as a facilitator of the key behaviours workshop is to support them.

Keep things moving! Keep sessions moving according to the times provided in this guide. Some groups will finish an exercise quicker than the others. Discuss with them the conclusions they have drawn. However, one area you should not be tempted to speed up is the start of each exercise. Once people have had a chance to understand what is required of them, the pace and level of discussion soon picks up. As the teams work, do not interfere. Intervene only when asked. Be on hand to help participant as soon as they seek your assistance, and ensure they can get your attention.

- Ensure that the participants think about how their conclusions translate into what they can do in their day-to-day roles.

Below are the key things you need to do and say as facilitator of a key behaviours workshop

Introduction
"As you can see mentioned in the key behaviours workshop fact sheet, a process and supporting materials have been developed with the objective of reaching all our employees so that they understand where we are moving to and the role they can have in supporting the change vision and key behaviours. During this meeting, we will be working together with this objective in mind. Your are grouped in groups of four to six people. Each group has a poster called key behaviours workshop.

"My role as facilitator is to:

- keep time,
- ensure the group keeps to the subject,
- clarify the conclusions that you have drawn,

- ensure everyone participates,
- and ensure that you and not I answer the questions we will ask.

"Indeed, there are no right or wrong answers. What is important is that we talk about your answers. You will get out of this workshop what you put in it.

"Let us look at the materials. Each of you has a participant guide. This is your personal guide. It includes the same exercises as the key behaviours workshop poster that you are being asked to fill in during the workshop, but from a personal, individual perspective. You will be asked at the start of each exercise to think individually about your answers and write them down in your guide.

After the workshop, we suggest you take this participant guide with you and regularly review it. The purpose of this workshop is to discuss as a team via a series of exercises the organisation's change ambition and key behaviours. Let me give you an overview of the things we will work on together as a team.

"At the top of this workshop there is a continuum, which reflects the different stages of implementing change. We start communicating the vision of change by looking at the organisation. What does the organisation want to be as a community? Who does the organisation want to be?

"We then turn the vision into reality and focus on the change vision's key behaviours. What common behaviours do we want to share as an organisation?

"Before setting milestones and acknowledging progress—by looking at what actions we can take to accelerate the speed of implementation of the vision of the change and the key behaviours—we look at how we respond to change. This will enable us to discover what obstacles can be anticipated, thus helping us prepare and anticipate actions to take.

"Finally, we will spend some time on building an action plan for the team and for each of you, to help accelerate the speed of implementation and make the organisation's ambition sustainable. I will introduce each exercise and then leave you to work in your small groups. You have pens on the table. These should be used to write the consensus you reach inside each group during the exercise. The whole process takes between three-and-half and four hours."

Ground Rules
"Before we start, a few ground rules for working in your groups:

- Switch off your mobile phone.
- Keep to the time.
- Actively contribute.
- Listen to others when they speak—don't interrupt.
- All ideas are valid—no right or wrong answers.
- The facilitator does not have the answer.
- All participants are equal."

First exercise: What are the key words?

Let's take a look at the organisation vision of the change X. In each group, take around fifteen minutes to agree on the key words of the organisation's ambition. First, take one minute to think alone about the answer to the question. Then, take five minutes to share and discuss inside the group and write on a piece of paper the answers that correspond to a consensus. Each participant writes down on a separate paper the answers that did not make it through the consensus phase.

We will then take two minutes per group to enable each group to share the consensus and the items that did not reach the consensus. Each group nominates a spokesman.

2nd exercise: What actions are we already taking in the organisation to support our vision?

In each group, take around fifteen minutes to agree about concrete examples. Think of what you are already doing and of what others are already doing. Think of examples from your team and examples from other teams of the organisation. It is very important that you provide concrete examples and use action verbs.

First, take two minutes to think alone about the answer to the question. Then take ten minutes to share and discuss inside the group, and write on the key behaviours workshop poster the answers that correspond to a consensus. Each participant writes down on a separate paper the answers that did not make it through the consensus phase.

We will then take two minutes per group to enable each group to share the consensus and the items that did not reach the consensus. Nominate a new spokesman for this exercise.

Note: It is probable that the participants will not only talk about how they are contributing today but also about what could be done in the future. This is okay. As a facilitator, you should suggest that some of these ideas be put into the action plan at the end of the key behaviours workshop.

3rd exercise: What does it mean for you?

In each group, take around fifteen minutes to agree about what the key behaviours mean for you. Think of examples from your team and examples from other teams of the organisation.

First, take two minutes to think alone about the answer to the question. Then take ten minutes to share and discuss inside the group and write on the key behaviours workshop poster the answers that correspond to a consensus. Each participant writes down on a separate paper the answers that did not make it through the consensus phase.

We will then take two minutes per group to enable each group to share the consensus and the items that did not reach the consensus. Nominate a new spokesman for this exercise.

Break (ten minutes)

During the break, start to think about how you can turn the key behaviours into real life day-to-day actions.

4th exercise: Assumptions and certainties

Each of us could interpret the key behaviours feasibility in different ways depending on our beliefs, certainties, and assumptions. We will now work on these underlying assumptions and certainties. In each group, take around fifteen minutes to discuss. What makes you think key behaviours are difficult or too early to adopt on a daily basis? What proofs or examples do you have that this is true? What examples are there of exceptions where the key behaviours where easy to adopt on a daily basis? For each of these three questions, think of examples from your team and examples from other teams of the organisation.

First, take six minutes to think alone about the answer to the three questions (two minutes per question). Then take ten minutes to share and discuss inside the group and write on the key behaviours workshop poster the answers that correspond to a consensus about the last question: Are there exceptions, during which the key behaviours were easy to adopt, on a daily basis? Each participant writes down on a separate paper the answers that did not make it through the consensus phase.

We will then take two minutes per group to enable each group to share the consensus and the items that did not reach the consensus. Nominate a new spokesman for this exercise.

5th exercise: How you can concretely demonstrate these key behaviours in your daily work

In each group, we will now take around fifteen minutes to agree about how each of you can demonstrate and live and breath according to these key behaviours. To answer this we will ask three questions. If I were to meet you in six months:

- How would I know that you are working according to the key behaviours?
- What are you saying or doing?
- What are others saying about you?

For each of these three questions, think of examples from your team and examples from other teams of the organisation.

First, take six minutes (two min. per question) to think alone about the answer to the three questions. If you so desire I can hand out a proposal of definitions behind each key behaviour that corresponds to what other organisations' members have proposed. Please see the appendix of your participant guide. This is not a definite or the right answer, but an example.

Then take twenty-five minutes (ten min. per subgroup + ten min. to share + five min. to agree on a consensus) to share and discuss inside the group, and write on the key behaviours workshop poster the answers that correspond to a consensus.

Since you need to cover all of the key behaviours, I suggest you divide yourselves into four subgroups of people working so that each of the key behaviours is addressed in parallel (not in sequence). Each participant writes on a separate paper the answers that did not make it through the consensus phase.

We will then take two minutes per group to enable each group to share the consensus and the items that did not reach the consensus. Nominate a new spokesman for this exercise.

We will focus on the next part of the key behaviours workshop dedicated to our emotional responses to a change.

As most of you probably know when something new comes along, people have different reactions. Some will see it positively, some less positively. Experience and research shows that when we are confronted to a change or something new, five emotional states have been identified. You can see them on the key behaviours workshop poster. We all necessarily pass through all five states when something new comes along. The difference between how people react to a specific change is the speed in which they pass through the phases. In addition, the length of the phase is not always the same for everyone; it depends of the topic of the change.

It is vital that each person is given the opportunity to digest each phase fully and is not forced to pass one of these phases. Otherwise he or she will fall back to the not fully digested phase when under pressure or confronted with difficulties to implement the change. This is why it is important that people talk about what they are experiencing, how it affects them, and how they can help one another to deal with it.

This journey of phases is seldom a smooth or linear sequence. However, the objective for the organisation is to get everybody at least to the acceptance state. How do you know in which emotional phase a person is in? By listening carefully to what they say.

For example:

- A person negatively shocked might say: "What?" "You must be joking!" No way!"
- A person positively shocked might say: "Wow!" "Finally!" "Great!"
- A person in denial might say, "This does not affect me!" "It will never work!" "It'll never happen!" "They're not key behaviour principles!"
- A person who is confused might say, "I don't understand what you're explaining." "Why can't they explain it more clearly?" "What's it got to do with me?" "How does this link to other initiatives?"
- A person in acceptance might say, "I think I can integrate it into my daily work." "It makes sense." "What can I do to help you implement this?" "I'm committed."
- A person in the problem solving might say, "I am going to make this work." "I have some great ideas."

As an example, think back to when you read the organisation's vision of change or key behaviours. What thoughts were in your head? Some of you may have thought: "Finally, the organisation is announcing its vision." "Great!" "It makes sense" and "I am committed." They are in the acceptance phase.

Others may have thought: "You must be joking." "Not another initiative." "It won't last long." "It will never work." They are in the denial or confusion phase. Being in a phase or another does not make you a good or bad employee. But staying stuck in a phase other than acceptance is something the organisation wants to avoid.

6th exercise: What emotional stage are we in

For a change to take place, we must have an understanding of a person's emotional stage. Depending of the emotional phase a person is in, he or she will need different types of supports from peers and colleagues in order to adopt a change.

Let's start a new exercise.

First, with regards to the key behaviours and vision, put an X in red for where you feel you were at the beginning of the workshop and in blue for where you feel you are now on the curve (five minutes)."

Note: This is not easy for everyone to complete. So do not force someone if he or she does not wish to express feelings. To de-dramatize, as facilitator, start by putting up two Xs first and explaining how you feel.

Once most participants have put their X say, "Remember the organisation's goal is to have all employees at the acceptance phase. So how do you help a person go from one phase to another?"
Experience and research shows that if people are in the phase of confusion, denial or shock, you could probably help them if you:

- Listen to them; give them to opportunity to voice their disagreements, feelings, and concerns.

- Explain why change is mandatory and why now.
- Give them a lot of information about what it feels and looks like once the change is implemented.
- Let them decide what their first step toward the desired change will be.
- Explain that the reasons for the change are to build on previous success and strengths (rather than a way to fix problems).
- Acknowledge that we know that changing will not be easy and that it is normal and healthy to first be a bit hesitant and want to understand before deciding to change.
- Communicate the benefits of changing, rather sanctions if one does not adapt to the change.
- Use new arguments to explain the reason for change, rather than repeating the same ones.
- Show there are many alternatives in terms of how to change, but that the fact of changing is non-negotiable.
- Share success stories of people having changed and benefited from doing so.

Experience and research shows that if people are in the acceptance phase you could probably help them sustain this phase or move to problem solving if you communicate time lines.

- Allow for mistakes.
- Celebrate first attempts to change.
- Communicate tips, methods and trainings on how to make the execution of the change easier.

Slim Lambert

- Repeat the same arguments for changing relentlessly (especially those related to "what's in it for you").
- Involve them in quick-wins and success stories.
- Communicate the fact that the individual changes should not be too stretching because if they are, there is risk of not reaching them.
- Share success stories of people having changed and benefited from doing so.
- Don't reward a change with money; reward it with recognition and additional choices or opportunities to progress or to benefit from resources and learning.

"Any questions? Let's move on to the second part of the exercise.

What needs to happen for all the members of this team to accept organisation's ambition and key behaviours? If the majority of participants of a group are in acceptance mode, then get the group to think about what actions need to take place to make the change sustainable.

In each group, take around fifteen minutes to agree on concrete examples. Think of examples from your team and examples from other teams of the organisation. First, take two minutes to think alone about the answer to the question. Then take ten minutes to share and discuss inside the group, and write on the key behaviours workshop poster the answers that correspond to a consensus. Each participant writes down on a separate paper the answers that did not make it through the consensus phase.

We will then take two minutes per group to enable each group to share the consensus and the items that did not reach the consensus. Nominate a new spokesman for this exercise."

7th exercise: What action plans?
"The objective here is to define actions that this team as a whole—not the groups of four to six people you have been in today in the workshop—should be taken on to accelerate the speed of adoption of the key behaviours and ambition.

These action need to be in the form of

- Start doing X.
- Continue doing X (because it adds value).
- Stop doing X.

In each group, take around fifteen minutes to agree on concrete examples. Think of examples from your team and examples from other teams of the organisation.

First, take two minutes to think alone about the answer to the question Then take ten minutes to share and discuss inside the group. Write on the Key Behaviours workshop poster the answers that correspond to a consensus. Each participant writes down on a separate paper the answers that did not make it through the consensus phase.

We will then take two minutes per group to enable each group to share the consensus and the items that did not reach the consensus. Nominate a new spokesman for this exercise."

Last exercise: "You"

"Think in terms of what *you* need to:

- start doing,
- continue doing (because it adds value),
- or stop doing.

"Write them down in your individual participant guide. Take around ten minutes to think of concrete things and steps of an action plan. If you so desire, take five minutes to share it with one of your neighbour and accept their comments."

Close the key behaviours workshop

These sessions can be tiring and people will be processing a significant amount of information at this stage. You may wish to lead a Q&A session at this point to answer some of the immediate questions that people have. However, it is also important that people take time to reflect quietly on the insights they have gained and what the session has meant for them.

As a conclusion, ask the participants to think about the following questions:

- What has today's session accomplished for you?
- What are the key insights you will take from participating in today's session?
- What can you and this team apply when you return to the workplace?

3.8. A TOOL FOR MANAGERS OR HRs, TO HELP THEIR TEAM MEMBERS DO THEIR INDIVIDUAL TRANSITION INTO THE NEW WAYS OF WORKING, DEFINED AS AN OUTPUT OF THE DIALOGUE WORKSHOPS.

3.8.1. *Overview*

Managers and human resource personnel who wish to help an employee align to the change can act as mentors or guides who use some coaching techniques. They then have one thing in common with professional coaches: they do not give the solution to the employee but rather help the employee build his or her own solutions.

Nevertheless, external coaches and these managers or HRs do not do the same things or use the same levers to help the person progress. A manager or HR focuses on the employee's environment whereas the professional coach focuses on the coaches. That is, the manager or HR helps the person by creating an environment that prompts him or her to find new ways of addressing the difficulties they face. The professional coach acts on how the person perceives his or her environment and he or she reacts to these perceptions. Messing around with perception is something that requires some specific interpersonal skills. The good news is that acting on the environment is as efficient, if not more so, than acting on the person's perceptions.

Slim Lambert

<u>1: As a manager or HR person, use listening skills to understand how the employee addresses the difficulty.</u>

<u>2: Help the employee gather feedback on how he or she addresses the difficulty.</u>

A questionnaire for self-assessment and assessment by stakeholders of the difficult situation the employee faces can be helpful. The questionnaire analyses the employee's intent to do try out new behaviours and the emotional reactions to doing this. This will characterize in six readiness levels.

Instruction:

Mr./Mrs....has as ambition to act differently when faced with the situation.... To what extent do following sentences apply to him.

For each sentence give a rating from 1 (does not apply to him or her) to 5 (applies perfectly to him or her)

1. Does not plan to change in the five months to come.
2. Rationalises—denies responsibility or possibility of acting differently.
3. Allots the responsibility of changing to others.
4. Allots the possibility to change on factors he or she does not control.

5. Denies the difficulty he or she faces in the situation.

6. Avoids the issue and the subject of changing.

7. Wishes above all to avoid criticism in the situation.

8. Has tried to change and is demoralised because of failure to do so.

9. Sometimes says, "It's not really possible to do differently."

10. Sometimes says, "I do not truly need to change."

11. Sometime says, "I know most of you don't think it's necessary for me to change."

12. Shows incredulity or does not accept reality—to some extent the "ostrich attitude."

13. Is learning and looking for information in order to change.

14. Thinks about changing, but not in the next twenty days, but rather in the next five months.

15. Has not engaged himself or herself publicly or vis-à-vis himself or herself to act differently.

16. Has mixed or ambivalent expressions such as, "I know that I should,.but..."

17. Awaits the perfect understanding of how to act differently, and until then will not change.

18. Wishes to act differently while preserving the advantages of his or her current ways of doing.

19. Focuses on the difficulty more than the solution to it.

20. Sometimes says, "Doing it differently will not work."

Slim Lambert

21. Sometimes says "I don't do the things I'm supposed to change."

22. Sometimes says, "I do not have the choice but to do as I'm currently doing."

23. Denies the necessity for him to act differently.

24. Continues to act as before.

25. Denies evidence old ways are harmful or unproductive.

26. Sees only the negative sides of the change or tends to exaggerate them.

27. Sometimes says, "I'll change later; it's not that urgent."

28. Has created and validated an action plan, including in the details of this plan.

29. Has made a choice between various solutions or options to act differently.

30. Has already made some small changes.

31. Has already "tried" at least once to act differently.

32. Has engaged him/herself publicly and toward him/herself to act differently

33. Doubts whether he r she will be able to implement the chosen new way of doing things.

34. Is uncertain of how others will react if he or she changes.

35. Seems frustrated by the necessity to change.

36. Sometimes asks, "Why is it me who has to change?"

37. Sometimes says, "It is not me; it's you who has a problem."

38. Sometime says, "The need for me to change is due to the general obsession to always want to change things that work well."

39. Sometimes asks, "Why don't just do my job and leave this change business to when I'll have nothing better to do?"

40. Seeks scapegoats to justify the need not to change.

41. Is cynical about the need to do things differently.

42. Feels guilty about not having had the good or new behaviour in the past.

43. Accepts that he or she could have been wrong in the past.

44. Tries to negotiate himself or herself out of needing to change.

45. Sometimes says the need to change will become irrelevant as times go by.

46. Has implemented the new ways of doing things since approximately five months.

47. Has set up a system of control to make his or her change supported by routines, habits, and others.

48. Sometimes seems apathetic or lacking the motivation to continue doing things differently.

49. Has changed, but sometimes mentions that it was unfair or not needing to change.

50. Sometimes regrets his or her old ways of doing things.

51. Does not go beyond doing the minimal change that he or she promised.

52. Has changed his or her act but not his or her mindset.

53. Sometimes relapses into old ways of doing things.

54. Has given up, since more than five months, the acts or behaviours that have been changed.

55. Actively prevents any relapse to old ways of doing things.

56. Is proud of having changed.

57. Does not accuse himself or herself of being wrong in the past; rather, thinks it was a rational behaviour at the time or the best he or she was able to do.

58. Is very excited about being able to do things differently.

59. The energy directed toward fighting against the change is now used for constructive creativity.

60. Looks to the future and not the past.

61. Reorganizes his other objectives, constraints, priorities in order to be able to benefit from the new ways of doing things.

62. He or she focuses energy on the best way of making the most out of the situation that represented a difficulty before.

63. Is not at all tempted by the old ways of doing

64. Would be frustrated if he or she stopped adopting the new behaviours.

65. The new ways of doing have become a normal thing to do.

3.8.3.   Step 2, help the employee analyse the feedback.

The purpose is to use the feedback to provide the employees with an increased understanding of how they are perceived by others and of the levers to become more effective in addressing the difficult situation. For the manager or HR, the purpose is to use the feedback as a building block for the choice of how to help the employee. Of course, the first step is to analyse the feedback in order to create a feeling of accountability in employee for their own progress. Feedback is a powerful yet sensitive process and one that needs an environment of reciprocal openness and trust to be successful.

The manager or HR could use the following script of sequential questioning

— "Before we look at the feedback let's not forget that:

o The focus is *how* you interact with others, not if you are right or wrong in your reactions.

o This feedback is the perception of others, not necessarily an absolute truth.

o The purpose is to transform this feedback into a development plan, not to judge you.

o We should refrain from getting so hung up on a couple of issues raised in the feedback to the point of overlooking the big picture.

— Do you agree?
— To understand the data, we should know that statements

1 to 12: correspond to Level 1 (the lowest level of readiness)
13 to 27: correspond to Level 2
28 to 45: correspond to Level 3

46 to 53: correspond to Level 4

54 to 65: correspond to Level 5 (the highest level of readiness)

- Let's give some meaning to the data. Okay?
- What does the feedback report tell you? What scores pleased or puzzled you?
- What do the differences between the respondent groups suggest? Why are there differences?
- Are your self-ratings higher or lower than respondents' ratings?
- What are the differences within respondent groups? Why are there differences do you think?
- What about the total score for each level of readiness? What does it say about your readiness to address the situation differently?
- What are your key assets in addressing the situation differently?
- What are the key messages from the different perspectives?
- Please fill in the following table:

	That which I will remember	That which I learned or discovered	That which was confirmed	That which I disagree with
About me				
About my intent to change				
About my emotions				

The manager or HR adopts a tactic of supports given to the employees according to their readiness level:

For level 1 of readiness
- Help the employees label their and other's emotions in the situation.
- Make the employees observe the situation without them being part of it and how others address the situation they face.
- Help the employees get feedback from as many different sources as possible.
- Work with employees on the purpose and types of defensive reaction somebody can have.
- Make the employees note down what they and others do in the situation.
- If possible make a role-play of the situation and make the employees act it out with you.
- Do not insist or try to convince the employees about the fact that doing things differently is necessary.
- Apply listening techniques described in tactic 1 again.
- Help the employees decompose the difficulty into small parts that are less difficult.
- Make the employees say that they do not see the utility of changing and explain why.
- Show that you fully trust that the employees would be able to change if they wanted.
- Praise the employees for current success and past changes they've made.
- Give as much information to the employees about the situation and the need to change the way they currently are doing things.

- Show what is funny in the situation because it constitutes a paradox.
- Make the employees interview stakeholders in the situation on the perceptions they have of theme and their impact on the stakeholders' feelings, thoughts, and reactions.

For the level 2 of readiness
- Help the employees label their and other's emotions in the situation.
- Make the employees observe the situation without them being part of it and how others address the situation they face.
- Be empathic to the fears, doubts, concerns the employees have about the fact of doing things in a new way.
- Listen, listen, listen—let the employees express their feelings until they do not feel the need to do so.
- Don't say that changing will be easy.
- Don't push the employees into changing; let them do it when they feel ready.
- Help the employees map out the pros, cons, risks, opportunities, and benefits that result from the change. Make it as if it is they who wants to convince you of the need to change.
- Show that you fully trust that the employees would be able to change and have the capabilities to do the new things.
- Give as much information to the employees about what the situation will look like after the change.
- Help the employees identify how the new things they will do are aligned to their own personal values.

<u>For the level 3 of readiness</u>

- Work with the employees on how to design an action plan, define an objective, and build a support for an action by others.
- Help the employees work on how the environment could nurture and sustain the change.
- Praise and be excited about the small steps made toward doings things differently.
- Encourage the employees to make additional efforts. Recognize these efforts in the way that makes the employees the most proud.
- If the employees relapse, do not judge them. Be emphatic and encourage them to try out new experiences.
- Lobby to create an environment (processes, rewards, mindsets) favourable of the new things the employees plan on doing.
- Create opportunities for the employees to test doing the new things in a risk-free context.
- Work with the employee to set up indicators of when they are not doing the new things.

<u>For the level 4 of readiness</u>

- Work with employees on avoiding any black and white thinking, such as good/bad, wrong/right, my fault/ their fault.
- Work with the employees on expressing emotions in a constructive manner and the triggers of positive or negative emotions.
- Act as if it is obvious, and prove this through your acts and decisions, that the employees will continue doing things differently

Slim Lambert

- Lobby to create an environment (processes, rewards, mindsets) favourable of the new things the employees plan on doing.

For the level 5 of readiness
- Make the employees aknowledge publicly to do the new things.
- Help the employees label their and other's emotions in the situation.
- Make the employees observe the situation without them being part of it and how others address the situation they face.
- Give the employees the opportunity to help others do the change they've done.
- Train the employees on skills useful to do even more fully the new things.
- Train the employees and give them advice on how not to relapse.
- Go beyond acts and work with the employees on their mindset.
- Make sure that employees do not get too pumped-up and define overly ambitious goals in doing the new things.
- Make sure the employees do not feel guilty if they relapse.
- Reward the employees one time, but significantly, for the change made.

The goals are:

- Launch sponsored projects that represent large-scale experiments to align the way things are done with the change vision.
- Provide to people who have not fully implemented initiatives of step 1 the opportunity to act in a new way.
- Make the change even more concrete and visible by translating it in transversal actions.
- Strengthen credibility of the change across the organisation.
- Strengthen the support for the change effort across the organisation.
- Demonstrate that progress is occurring across the organisation.
- Strengthen support from people in positions of power or influence across the organisation.
- Strengthen momentum for the change effort with more people becoming active contributors and helpers.
- Infuse energy in the change management process and attention through "hot groups," which I will define later.
- Infuse a sense of excitement as people *see* change happening, feel the momentum, and want to act.

- Provide sponsoring aimed at ensuring that the first steps of a project change the organisation and are as easy as possible for the employees.
- Officially restate that experimentation is allowed.
- Get employees doing something differently that embeds the change, even for some trivial reason or because it is asked of them by their peers who drive the project.

Then the organisation helps them explain, through communication about success stories, why it is important and why they are doing it. Indeed, when people buy into doing small things, the organisation can get them doing increasingly significant things. People have a deep need for congruence, and when they do something, they need to have consistency and alignment between their actions and their beliefs. When there is inconsistency, they either change what they are doing or what they believe in order to restore consistency and congruence. If they have already started doing something, then they cannot change what has been done, so they must change what they believe.

Another reason for consistency is that they worry about that others think about them will be confused and reject them as they transgress that was before expected of them. They thus have a strong need to explain to them what they are doing. This works internally, too, and they tell themselves the reasons for their actions. It is important that the person is unable to rationalise why they acted in this way by thinking about the encouragement they were given. So, in this step of the change process people should not be paid or commanded to act, otherwise they may rationalise that they did it for the money or the boss, not because they really believed it was the right thing to do.

- Provide a large amount or dramatic evidence of why the change is needed.

Cold, hard data is difficult to ignore at the step of the individual change people are at this step of the REFRESHING change management process. The data needs to be destabilizing. It needs to shake employees of their comfort zone.

- Maintain the sense of urgency established in the previous steps of the change management process.
- Build the communities of practice around the new role, expertise, and ways of working.
- Set stretch goals.
- Provide evidence that the plan for change is working.
- Provide tangible results to help keep leaders and stakeholders on board as well as undermine resisters and silence the cynics.
- Provide a chance to catch your breath and celebrate—to make a tough journey more tolerable.

3.9.1. How does this differ from the change management's classic approach to launching pilots?

These projects are not pilots as defined in classic change management approaches because they:

- are launched while the change has already been implemented locally;
- are not defined from scratch; (They are duplicate, replications, mergers, extensions, translations of actions proposed after step 1 or the let go step.)
- are set up to accelerate and embed the change, not prove its feasibility;
- are under the responsibility of the leader responsible for the project. (But the components of the projects are proposed by the people.)
- are done using "hot groups," (which I will describe in the following paragraphs).

3.9.2. How does the leader select the projects to sponsor?

The leader coordinates the assessment of proposed projects. The assessment is made by a representative panel of the organisation and is based on the following criteria rated on a scale from -5 to +5:

- How fast could it realistically be done?
- How much effort and expense will it take? How easy is it to implement?

- How unambiguous will the result be?
- How visible will the result be? (How factual will it be?)
- Will this be viewed as a meaningful win? (Why?)
- How meaningful will it be to people with formal or informal power to influence people's mindsets?
- How much does it target results rather than activities?
- How much does it embed the change, accelerate it, or sustain it?
- How much does it act on the culture?
- How much does it open the way for other projects that will be useful for the change?
- How much does it reorganize to break up cosy groups (i.e., those aligned to the change but do not drive it)?
- How timely is the project (i.e., how does it serve current business priorities in addition to those of the change)?
- How relevant is the project to the people who need to carry the change forward?

Then, given these assessments, the leader coordinates the identification of:

- Short term projects.

Here you are looking for quick wins and immediate results. Efforts should focus on short-term wins that are the easiest to achieve with the biggest payoff. You may also choose to target some of the easy ones that have a smaller payoff. These short-term projects do not necessarily need to be earthshaking. But they need to be big enough to inspire the driving forces and to silence the resisting forces. Short-term projects build the credibility of the plan for change. These projects also turn neutrals into supporters.

- Long term projects.

Here you are looking at projects that will profoundly and permanently change "the way we do things around here."

3.9.3. *Why is a step of the change methodology dedicated to sponsoring action? Do you not think that employees will act now that they have the desire and commitment to change?*

Preparation is an important stage in the change process, but it is also fraught with danger. If you've ever been part of an organisation that engages in endless planning with little or no action to show for it, you've seen the dangers of preparation first hand. It is very easy for the preparation to become the activity. Planning doesn't actually change anything.

At the sponsoring of projects step, it is time to make decisions about what actions to take that can sustainably and definitely change the organisation. It is especially aimed for people not directly or fully at the origin of step 1 actions.

Analysis paralysis can be a factor in this step of the process. Indeed, there are usually many possible ways to create change, and often one method is just as valid as another. Sponsoring ensures that there is just enough planning, not a bit more. It is critical to remain focused on the desired change more than the path to getting there, or procrastination can again take over.

Why is action is the hardest part of change? Human beings are really good at procrastinating. It's such an issue that there is an entire industry churning out motivational material, affirmations, and even ways to outsource all of the things that you're going to procrastinate anyway! Yet we still continue to avoid taking actions that we truly think will be helpful to us. And you are not immune to the procrastination bug even though you are well aware of the psychology that causes it. There are a few common reasons for this: fear of failure, fear of success, the stuff seems hard, or the initial step of getting the train going can be really daunting. Then the need for congruence takes over and drives movements and actions of people and the organisation.

How do you avoid this paralysis by analysis? Don't try to build the perfect plan. Because plans rarely work out the way they were written, it is not helpful to aim for perfection in any planning process. You can always test and tweak your plan as you go along. The key is just to get started. Create the very roughest outline of a plan. When you find flaws in the plan, simply adjust and keep moving. So what if your first attempt fails? The key here is to learn and keep trying. Think short term. Commit to acting on your plan for a month, six months, or a year—whatever feels manageable to you. After the end of your time line evaluate your results and commit to more time if you wish. Realise that a plan isn't a life commitment, that it is sure to have weaknesses and will need adjustment over time. Minimize planning time and get into the excitement of action! Find ways to break up the change into small steps.

A hot group is a group totally focused on resolving a new or difficult challenge through experimentation during a short period of time. Hot groups are guerrilla warriors, moving, changing, and doing what needs to be done, then disappearing.

They address a cross-company task and are given an unusual amount of leeway and power. Members work full-time for a few months. People are taken off their jobs and put on this time for six weeks, full time, or part time. They have the right to talk to anybody they want, do anything they want, and operate with few boundaries.

They typically bond and listen more carefully to each other for the first time. They also become candid with one another. As a group, they become more daring than any individual. They address problems and look for solutions in a way that wouldn't normally happen on the job. You give them permission to be very creative and bold. Not all do so, but in some cases, it's marvellous.

Hot groups gather a broad range of data. There is no "Well, yes, but the chairman is out those three weeks." There is no "Don't stir the waters too much; be practical. Make sure ideas can be implemented; make sure the ideas are so trivial that no one will try to block them."

A hot group is a state of mind, not a name for some new kind of team or task force or committee. The hot group state of mind is

Slim Lambert

task-obsessed and full of passion. To illustrate, strangely, while hot groups are not welcome, "teamwork" is. Is it a paradox? Hardly! The word "teamwork" usually has little to do with hot groups. In practice, praising someone as a good "team player" often means someone who obediently conforms to his or her senior's expectations.

You could consider the hot group as a meeting tool of the REFRESHING change management process that never ends and includes ad-hoc participants as needed.

Not everyone works well in a hot group. You need people who are willing. You can't coerce people into doing something like this. They also have to have the knowledge or base of experience to work on the problem. They need to be willing to challenge the status quo for good reasons, to ask why, and to question the rules instead of just accepting what is set in stone because it's always been done that way. And they need to be able to leave their desk with the agreement that they won't be back until the solution is found. This last point is a real challenge because the types of people we need in a hot group are typically not those who are easy to free up. This is where the leader needs to step in to free them up if needed.

One of the reasons that make hot groups key is that *somewhere in the waves of change, you will have to attack the sturdy silos and difficult politics or you won't create a twenty-first-century organisation.* In the early stages of a change, the silos and politics can be too tough to handle. But eventually, you must choose to deal with this heavy lifting or you will never fulfil the vision. The sponsored projects step of the change is a good time to launch hot groups.

An after action review (AAR) is a discussion of a project or an activity that enables the individuals involved to learn for themselves what happened, why it happened, what went well, what needs improvement, and what lessons can be learned from the experience. It is a key input for storytelling (I will come back to this later). The spirit of an AAR is one of openness and learning—it is not about problem solving or allocating blame. Lessons learned are not only tacitly shared on the spot by the individuals involved, but they can be explicitly documented and shared with a wider audience. AARs are excellent for making tacit knowledge explicit after a project. *This meeting may take place over a couple of hours or a couple of days, depending on the scale of the project.*

Questions to address are:

- What where the objectives and deliverables of the project?

Ask, What did we set out to do? What did we actually achieve? What was supposed to happen? What was the objective of the piece of work? Was there a clear objective? What actually happened? What was the result? What was supposed to happen? You might also decide to construct a flow chart of what happened, identifying tasks, deliverables, and decision points (this can help you to see which parts of the project were particularly effective or ineffective).

Slim Lambert

- What did we learn?

Ask, What went well? Find out why, and share learning advice for the future. It is always a good idea to start with the positive points. Here you are looking to build on best practice as well as learn from mistakes. For each point that is made about what went well, keep asking a why question. This will allow you to get to the root of the reason. Then press participants for specific, repeatable advice that others could apply in similar situations.

- What could have gone better?

Find out what the problems were, and share learning advice for the future. Notice that you are not simply asking what went wrong but rather what could have gone better. This way you can learn not only from mistakes, but also from aspects of the project that got in the way of delivering even more. Hence, the focus is not on failure but on improvement. Even if no mistakes are made, there is almost always room for improvement. Again, for each point that is made, keep asking a why question to get to the root of the reason. Then again press participants for specific, repeatable advice that others could apply in similar situations—what would they do differently next time?

- Summarize the AAR in order to share the projects in the form of a story.

It is important to have a clear and interesting account of the AAR and its learning points, both as a reminder to those involved and in order to share that learning with others effectively. You should aim to include things like lessons and guidelines for the future, some background information about the project to help put these guidelines into a meaningful context, the names of the people involved for future reference, and any key documents such as project plans or reports.

Some advice:
Any other use of the candid discussions that take place must be strictly prohibited. In fact, using input from an AAR for any other purpose, including performance evaluations, is a career-ending event. The focus is on what can be learned, not who can be blamed. Expect people to learn from the mistakes and not make the same mistake twice. Learning is expected.

Some ground rules:
Do not try to judge success or failure.

Learn *why* things happened.

Focus on the tasks and goals that were supposed to happen.

Encourage people to surface important issues and lessons.

Have as many people as possible participate.

Learn about what matters.

Use facilitators who coach and don't lecture.

3.11.1.   Why use after action review as a basis for storytelling?

Stories represent one of the greatest tools at any communicator's disposal. When used correctly, stories can be powerful in their ability to bring people together around a common purpose. The best stories are usually discovered rather than manufactured. Stories that are designed to manipulate stakeholders to behave in a certain way often elicit the opposite effect. Storytelling works best when it is the product of an ongoing dialogue between the organisation and its people. This is the case when the stories are the results of the AAR. Be aware—what the leader cares about does not tap into roughly 80 percent of the workforce's primary motivators for putting extra energy into the change program. This is taken into account if the elements of a story are the outputs of the AAR.

Why form the lessons learned from the AAR into a story? *Good stories are more powerful than plain facts.* This is not to reject the value of facts, of course, but simply to recognize their limits in influencing people. People make decisions based on what facts mean to them, not on the facts themselves. Stories give facts meaning. Stories resonate with adults in ways that can bring them back to a childlike open-mindedness and make them less resistant to experimentation and change.

What are the levers of storytelling? Why does it work? *It doesn't replace analytical thinking. It supplements it by enabling us to imagine new perspectives and new worlds.* It is ideally suited to communicating change and stimulating innovative solutions embedded in the change. Abstract analysis is easier to understand when seen through the lens of a well-chosen story and can of course be used to make explicit the implications of a story.

I do not recommend abandoning abstract thinking, nor do I suggest that we should give up the advances that have emerged through experimentation and science. I suggest marrying the communicative and imaginative strengths of storytelling with the advantages of abstract and scientific analysis. Research by leading thinkers in the social sciences such as Danah Zohar has shown that when managers and employees are asked what motivates them the most in their work, they are equally split among five forms of impact—impact on society (for instance, building the community and stewarding resources), impact on the customer (for example, providing superior service), impact on the company and its shareholders, impact on the working team (for example, creating a caring environment), and impact on "me" personally (my development, pay check, and bonus). If change leaders are to be able to tell a change story that covers all five things that motivate employees, they can unleash tremendous amounts of energy that would otherwise remain latent in the organisation.

Stories are vehicles for learning. Before learning can take place, there must be an interest. Abstract principles and impersonal procedures are not attractive. However, everyone likes a good story.

Stories are capable of conveying a rich and clear message. They provide an example in a non-threatening manner. Moreover, stories are memorable. The messages stemming from a particular story tend to stick. Stories fill our lives in the way that water fills the lives of fish. Stories are so all-pervasive that we practically

Slim Lambert

cease to be aware of them. We create narrative descriptions for ourselves and for others about our own past actions and develop storied accounts that give sense to the behaviour of others. We also use the narrative scheme to inform our decisions by constructing imaginative "what if" scenarios.

Stories spark thoughts among the listener about a different kind of futures both for the organisation and for himself or herself as an individual. Stories stimulate the listeners to think actively about the implications of the doing things differently and what it will be like to be doing things in a different way.

Stories enable listeners to grasp an idea in a non-threatening way. It invites them to see analogies from their own backgrounds, their own contexts, their own fields of expertise. The listener makes analogies while listening. Stories are vectors to engage the listener in an exercise of stimulating the imagination. This exercise will pull the listener into exploring different representations or perceptions of a given situation; creating association and dissociations of ideas; suspending value judgments; abandoning, for a brief moment, rationalizations made; and reframing the meaning of a situation. What is unique with stories is that the storyteller does not push but pulls, or rather lets the listener fill the gaps that the stories leave open. This is because listeners, while listening to the story, are still connected to the "what's in for me radio." There is a projection and an identification—one that is spontaneous and voluntary (without the storyteller needing to ask the listeners to project themselves into the protagonist of the story). The story becomes the listener's one. Because the listener imaginatively recreates the story in his or her own mind, the story is not something foreign, not something perceived as coming from outside, but rather something that is perceived as part of the listener's own identity. *The listener is not a passive receiver of information, but is triggered into a state of active thinking.*

Contrary to facts, the levers of stories lever are emotions, imagination and mental visualization. Therefore they offer a direct route to the heart (and thus not only make the listener do things, but do it with energy and enthusiasm). What truly moves us as human beings, what prompts us into action, are emotions and visualization. Imagination is the conduit of emotion and well-crafted storytelling carries the imagination. Facts tell. Emotion sells.

3.11.2. How do you build stories about change agents and sponsored projects?

Tip 1. How to structure a story.

A story does not have to cover each of the following items, but an effective story will need to cover the majority of these.

The structure of a story should be sequenced as follows:

A balanced situation: "You come to work day after day, week after week, and everything's fine."

An incident: Then there's an event or incident that throws life out of balance: "You get a new job, or the boss dies of a heart attack, or a big customer threatens to leave."

The desire: The protagonist has a desire to find a solution to restore the balanced situation. Desire is the blood of a story. Desire is not a shopping list but a core need.

The antagonist: Forces that keeps this need from being satisfied can be from within: doubt, fear, confusion, personal conflicts with friends/family/lovers. It can be external forces: social conflicts arising in various institutions in society, the forces of Mother Nature, not enough time to get things done, and the damn automobile that won't start.

The struggle to solve the conflict between the protagonist's desire and cruel reality: The storyteller describes what it is like to deal with these opposing forces and how the protagonist has to dig deep and reveal his or her true character and how to solve the dilemmas or make the choice. For example, it could be to work with scarce resources, make difficult decisions, take action despite risks, deal with the dark side of human beings, and so on.

The storyteller describes how the protagonist goes through a series of small triumphs that contribute to the final triumph. Hence, a four-part formula for telling stories is:

somebody...(a person, actor, group)
wanted...(what this person sought, desired, yearned for)

but...(complication, obstacle, conflict)

so...(resolution, climax, outcome, learning).

Tip 2. How to structure a story in order to explain and to make concrete values or principles.

1. Make the story in the form of a parable or metaphor to illustrate the conflict of values.
2. Set the story in some generic past and give few context or setting details (though the context needs to be relevant to the listener). The lack of details makes the listener imagine them.
3. Set the story in some kind of timeless past.
4. Tell a story about someone the listener admires.
5. The facts can be hypothetical, but they must be believable.
6. Create a rich visual imagery in the minds of the listeners and make it invite them to walk the landscape that is created by this imagery.

Tip 3. How to make a story memorable and make it stick.

By "stick" we mean that the story and its message are understood and remembered, and have a lasting impact (i.e., they change the audience's opinions and behaviours).

Start with an explicit proverb-like message that will be the first thing said by the storyteller. This is the essential core of the underlying idea that the story vehicles. A proverb is a one-sentence statement that is simple and profound enough that an individual could spend a lifetime learning to follow it. Assume that this will be the only thing that will be remembered

The content of the story/anecdote should: Set the context in a short manner, and contain analogies ("it's like...") in order to make the story short and link it to something the listener knows already.

Get the listener's attention through unexpectedness; surprise the listener. It must violate people's expectations and be counterintuitive enough to generate interest and curiosity. It should present a need to make a choice and the choice made should be unexpected. It should break a pattern of behaviour, attack an unspoken assumption or question the obvious and expected.

Common sense is the enemy of sticky messages. Keep the listener interested. It must progressively create an insight. After creating doubt, it must give an answer that enables the listener to restore predictability at the end of the story. The story is a road toward solving the mystery created by the unexpected. The unexpected has posed a question and opened a situation (the listener should ask a question such as, How will it turn out?).

Describe what the protagonist does in a language that is concrete, which uses familiar words and a lot of details. This will enable the listener to visualise the story. Remember, we humans believe what we see or feel—because this proves that it is true—and we only believe proof!

Now that the listeners believe the story, make them care about the message of the story. Remember, for people to act, they have to care. Ensure that when visualising, the listeners feel an emotion that they are naturally inclined to feel. Associate the message of the story with something the listeners already care about. To do this, evoke their self-interest by spelling out the benefits of aligning to the message, and evoke principles or rules of the group of people the listeners feel they belong to.

Sharing the stories. A Web site could be built for people to vote on the anecdotes they think best illustrate each of the changes. Try to make as many employees as possible share the stories with their peers.

3.12. What are the objectives of the step 'burning bridges'?

You want to reinforce the change, sustain it through the alignment of the organisational culture and work processes. This will act as if you were burning bridges and make it impossible for people to go back to the old ways of doing things.

The objective is to normalize and to sustain changes implemented so far. People are taken from a state of being in transition and moved to a stable state where the implemented change is now considered business as usual.

You want to avoid relapse to the old ways of doing things. So you put new systems and routines in place to make it easier to remain on the new path defined by the change. This is where a change becomes a habit or standard operating procedure.

For many changes, relapse is a real possibility, so this step is crucial. Employees have done all of the hard work of creating change. They've taken action and stuck with it long enough for the change to become a part of daily life. It is then that the relapse risk starts. It continues until you are ready to make a change to something that will replace your new status quo.

Beware! Most changes require ongoing maintenance. The challenge is *to make the change stick!* In a lot of ways, this step is the most difficult because it can seem like a long and difficult task to maintain a new habit or an organisational change over the long haul. Of course, the implemented change gets easier to maintain over time.

You want to nurture new actions that reinforce the change. This can be done in several ways. In a nutshell, you burn the bridges and *align the formal processes and the culture of the organisation.* By process, I mean the system that formally structures work related actions for people, such as policies, governance, processes, supportive tools, workflows, roles, and job descriptions. It is also people management policies such as recruitment, promotion, potential, and performance criteria that consider the desired change as a prerequisite for being normal or average (you do not want the desired change be perceived as being what characterises the exceptional few). Similarly, management processes such as goal setting, recognition and rewards, budgeting, and measurement of performance have to be changed to be consistent with the objectives of the new environment. It institutionalizes the changes. Even more importantly, it creates peer pressure because it generalizes the changed ways of working to all. It is tricky since what counts the most is the informal impact of a formal process, not the formal process. *Whatever you do, people will create a margin of manoeuvre for themselves when faced with a formal rule.* This gives them power, freedom, and social identity. Changes in the formal and informal organisational patterns must be considered and developed in concert with one another.

When changes have yet to be embedded in to the organisation's operations and culture, their success is far from guaranteed. *There is also a risk that the change effort will simply run out of gas and the momentum will grind to a halt.* With each passing day, it gets harder to generate the energy it takes to keep working at change. The messages become repetitious, the audiences less excited, the issues less strategic and more mundane. Indeed, we like to keep score, declare winners, and move on to the next game.

Burning bridges is also achieved by launching a new change that builds on now implemented changes. This new change builds on or compliments the change already made. *In a funny way, this new change can change formal processes and the corporate culture.* This new change is building on the fact that the previous one is taken for granted.

3.12.1. Why finish the change process with alignment of processes?

Because *if you start changing processes (and culture), that's a sure way to create resistance!* It's too important, too concrete, too much part of the day-to-day levers of engagement, too much influencing people's condition of success, and so on, to be imposed on people.

And, even more importantly, it is only once you have discovered and tried out the solutions embedded in the change that you can discover what culture and process environment is needed.

The approach is to start with the formal and informal realities of what the processes mean to change for people. And then, only afterward, decide what to do to align formal processes. And finally, align organisational structures of roles and responsibilities.

To do that, a key lever is the cascading of the workshop called Best Place to Work. The workshop focuses on the immediate impacts of the change on the day-to-day ways people do their job and their possibilities to be happy doing their job. This is key because the most stable thing in a company is the relationships people have toward their job and others in their daily context. These are the ingredients of what makes a job engaging.

So consolidating the things that make the job engaging, in the context and mindset of the implemented change, ensures or at least facilitates the change stickiness. When I say "most stable," I mean hardest to change once defined. Some say that culture, processes, or organisational structures are the most stable part of an organisational system and, therefore, one of the hardest things to change. However, cultures are created and changed by people. They change it in order to be comfortable or happy with their everyday work. *Of course, organisations can attempt to change these things, but it is still the people who implement that attempt based on their willingness to live with it.*

A thing that is unique in the cascading of the Best Place to Work workshops is that it is a bottom-up cascading process to redesign processes and structures. As bottom-up suggestions are made, you have the input for the later redesign of processes that are aligned to the informal and formal everyday life of the people. However it is not a simple bottom-up process, as I will detail in the next paragraphs.

3.12.3. On what should the action plan to align processes focus on, in addition to cascading the Best Place to Work workshop?

Remember that a process is a collection of related activities that adds value to a product or service for which a customer would be willing to pay. A process accomplishes specific objectives. It may require information in the form of specifications, instructions, and schedules. A process is a collection of activities that takes one or more kinds of input and creates an output that is of value to the customer.

The focus of your alignment of process is defined by two questions to ask yourself:

First, if we take the change for granted, which processes enable us to do things better, cheaper, faster? Once you've identified the processes that have the most leveraging impact, you address each process using habitual process improvement approaches.

Second, what information, knowledge flows, information processing, grouping, and linking would sustain the change?

Think of information collection, transfer of information, knowledge building, transfer of knowledge, transfer of a product from a work unit to another, feedback loops, the immediate internal customer, and the final customer.

Should the goal be to create new processes to use the existing processes? *The focus should be on recombining the best of existing processes.* Destroying existing processes and creating new ones means that employees have to cope with two time-consuming tasks simultaneously. Using whole existing, or parts of existing, processes requires mainly adapting to existing constraints or changing these constraints. Most often, the thing you are looking for is already used elsewhere in the organisation, especially after the previous steps of the change process. You probably have to think outside of the box and inspire yourself from manufacturing while working in marketing, for example. You can adopt two approaches. Means to an end—particular process recombinants that could serve the end of solving a business problem. Or ends for means—looking at one or more existing processes as recombinable means and deciding what end or opportunities they could serve to exploit.

What about communities of practice or interest? How can they be leveraged? Should they be sponsored or created? Networks such as communities of actions, practices, and interests represent the real way information is shared, knowledge is built, and people support each other on a daily basis. They emerge naturally, serendipitously, and informally. By essence, they cannot be created from scratch but only nurtured. Frequently, networks emerge because the formal structure of the firm does not provide the supports necessary to carry out work. The most realistic action, and the one with the highest return of investment, is, therefore, to recombine existing networks. These networks interlink many individuals in an organisation. The networks can be reused, redeployed, and recombined to sustain the change.

I have watched many attempts to create communities of practices. People start with the best intentions. However, unless there is real return to each community member for taking the time in their busy work life to give and take from the community, enthusiasm dissipates rapidly. So it is better to simply to let organisational networks do their job. Use an existing means for a brand new end. The question to ask is, how can we leverage these spontaneously emerging networks to solve new problem or skills needs prompted by the change? Often the simple fact of identifying the individuals who have these newly required skills and helping them build a network around them is an easy and efficient strategy. Sometimes these people can be asked to change roles in the organisation to get close to those who now need the new skill or can be recognized formally for their expertise and asked to develop these skills in other people.

Another strategy is to support the existing networks by formally allocating them resources or additional time for their community activities. You can also propose to the community to resolve some issues prompted by the change and formally state that their proposal will be acted on using "formal" resources. Recombining or merging networks by making them work together on an issue prompted by the change is another way to build on existing networks. You could also reproduce another person's network by having the original networker introduce a person to all his or her network contacts and vouch for the new person's trustworthiness. How do you identify the useful networks to address and issues prompted by the change? The key tool here is social network analysis. It is the mapping of a person's network. It indicates different types of relationships and patterns between different types of people. It can be done automatically using a questionnaire and a tool or even created automatically using, for example, the analysis of your Lotus Notes activities. A lot of tools are available on the market these days.

3.12.4. *Why focus on culture?*

First, changing structures and processes requires changes in the mindset, values, and behaviour of the organisation's members. *Processes can be applied in different manners* depending of the mindset of people, and they do not define the day-to-day habitual acts and behaviours of people. Change is about the latest.

Second, *the mindset is the glue of change*. The cultural system cannot be easily seen or touched, yet it is there all the same. And more importantly the people in the organisation know it very well. The law of the culture often outweighs any other law. In many organisations, it may be the strongest message of all.

The question to ask is, *What part of the culture can be reinforced in order to sustain the change?*

3.12.5.   *How do you define organisational culture?*

Culture is a system for differentiating between in-group and out-group people. It is created when people get together. It tells us how to behave and agree in a group. It is a system of collectively held values. It defines in a basic taken-for-granted fashion an organisation's view of itself and its environment.

When a group of people are to exist together, they need a set of rules that helps everyone know what to do in various circumstances, from arguing with one another to dealing with outsiders. These rules help to propagate the shared meaning and use the systems of meaning to make sense of what is happening and what is done. These rules are passed from one generation to the next because they are believed to be *useful for survival and adaptation.* Every organisation has its own way of doing things that influences virtually every aspect of working life (from how long coffee breaks are to how products and services are sold).

Organisational culture refers to the underlying values, beliefs, and principles that serve as a foundation for an organisation's management system, as well as the set of management practices and behaviours that both exemplify and reinforce those basic principles. Some aspects of organisational culture, such as individual behaviour and group norms, are very *visible.* "Working hard," "dressing conservatively," or "acting friendly to customers" are aspects of culture that are easy to observe. Other aspects of culture are harder to observe, since they represent *invisible* assumptions, values, and core beliefs. For example the belief in the importance of "doing things right the first time," "being honest and ethical in all transactions," or "going beyond expectations to satisfy the customer." This aspect of an organisational culture is the most efficient lever to act on, defined as the first lever of the inference ladder.

3.12.6. *Should you define the values that sustain the change from scratch?*

No. You want to clarify existing values that should be strengthened. It should represent a blend of those principles from your past that you want to preserve and the beliefs that you will need to share as you look to the future created by the change. You want to revive and recombine historical values, not define new ones. Building on existing values is the surest and fastest way to a culture change. You need to find new ends that can serve and de-emphasize the others. Or you can add a new axis of value to combine with an existing value. For example, add "control" to "risk taking" and it becomes "controlled risk taking."

Values are three to four words or short phrases (five words or less) that you can use as verbal pegs to cluster or summarize many of the related values at the top of your values hierarchy. They are the central hooks on which to hang the key behaviours defined in the change vision. They shape everyone's actions. Experience shows that a good way is to have values that are defined both in the form of "enable/do/create…" and "avoid…."

People cannot be asked to change their values or culturally linked elements before their beliefs have evolved and especially not before they are convinced through experimentation that the change is relevant. This would not be fair or realistic! *Changing a culture is consequence, not a prerequisite.* Why?

First, culture is about continuous negotiation. Culture is built from inside a group, not from outside pressure. Culture is not a static thing but something that everyone is constantly creating, affirming, and expressing. You cannot *make* an organisation's culture. Culture is being created all the time by everybody. Culture is the *result* of all the daily conversations and negotiations between the members of an organisation. They are continually agreeing (sometimes explicitly, usually tacitly) about the "proper" way to do things, and how to make meaning of the events of the world around them. If you want to change a culture, you have to change these conversations. It is what has happened during the previous steps of the REFRESHING change process.

Second, culture is created through solution finding. Solutions that repeatedly appear to solve problems tend to become part of the culture. The longer the solution seems to work, the more deeply it becomes embedded in the culture. *That is why you need to act on the culture only after solutions that are embedded by the change have been tried out for a while.* Much money has been spent on devising corporate values and teaching them to employees—most of it wasted. Why? Usually because the new values are aspirations totally unconnected from the reality of organisational life, that is, what employees know and understand about the way the organisation really is. Culture and values must be built on the reality of organisational success, not on its promise. Overt victories of the change are the foundation for expressing and spreading new values throughout the organisation. When the underlying reality has changed and people witness its success, that is the time to link new values to the emotional experience of winning. Culture is the *result* of all the daily conversations and negotiations between the members of an organisation. They are continually agreeing (sometimes explicitly, usually tacitly) about the "proper" way to do things, and how to make meanings about the events of the world around them.

Most change programmes try to effect change by looking first at structures, systems, and processes. Experience shows us that these initiatives usually have a limited success. A lot of energy (and money) is put into the programme to change cultures, with all the usual communication exercises, consultations, workshops, and so on. In the first few months, things seem to be changing, but gradually the novelty and impetus wears off and the organisation settles back into something like its previous configuration. The reason for this is that unless the paradigm of values at the heart of the culture is changed, there will be no lasting change. The paradigm of values is the first level of the inference ladder that members of a group use every second of the day. It is this lever that is the most efficient for addressing a culture. Peter Senge has described the "Ladder of Inference," which is based on the inner confidence that "our map of the reality is the truth," and "the truth is obvious" as a sequence of cognitive steps—we receive data through our senses (observation); we select data from what we observe (filter, subtraction); we add meaning to the data (colour, augmentation); we draw assumptions on the basis of the selected data and the meaning we added; we adopt beliefs (mental models) about the reality, and continue to select data (as per step 2) that correspond to these beliefs; and we act on our beliefs. So the complexity of the environment is "destroyed" by chunking it down in ways that are recommended in order to sustain the change. The richness of the environment means that processing all available information is impossible—there is simply too much of it. Reducing the tremendous amount of input from the environment actually reassures the people and makes their life simpler, so they often follow it. This is especially true when this is done at the end of the change process as we recommend in our methodology. *The point is that before this last step of the change process, the change management actions have progressively acted on people's inference ladder.* What you want to do now is to consolidate the first level of the ladder: the paradigm of values. A paradigm of values is a self-consistent set of ideas and beliefs, which acts as a filter, influencing how we perceive and how we make sense. This paradigm has a major effect on our perceptions and inferences. This paradigm of values encourages certain types of behaviour. If everyone believes there is a blame culture, it is much more likely that people will behave in blaming ways; in a similar situation, in a forgiveness culture people would be more likely to act in a constructive and encouraging way. Paradigm tends to be self-sustaining. A paradigm is like a self-fulfilling prophecy; there is a kind of circular logic attached to it, which makes it hard to break. Without paradigms of values to help us order and make sense of the world, we would be faced with an overwhelming mass of incoming data. It would be impossible to do even the most simple of day-to-day tasks without having to work everything out from first principles each time. It is the very fact that a paradigm acts as a filter that helps make life manageable and gives us a sense of stability in a changeable world.

So where do paradigms come from? They are not imposed by chief executives nor invented by consultants; rather, they *emerge* from a multiplicity of interactions between the individuals within the community. This has been done during the previous steps of the change process.

Third, you change a culture with stories. And before this last step, you probably don't have enough stories to be convincing about changing values and cultural elements. Stories convey your culture simply and reliably. If you want to change the culture, you have to change the stories that employees spontaneously and informally share between them.

Fourth, when an organisation is in a trouble it has to go through the gut-wrenching actions so common at the start of transformation. For example, laying off workers, cutting out layers of hierarchy, fixing the finances, changing processes and people's jobs, and making huge demands on their time and energy—attempts to build new values will fail if they follow close on the heels of actions that inevitably trigger negative emotions (shame, fear, anger, frustration).

Best practices state that there are six primary embedding mechanisms and six reinforcing mechanisms. The six primary embedding mechanisms are:

1. what leaders pay attention to, measure, and control;
2. how leaders react to critical incidents and crises;
3. how scarce resources are allocated;
4. deliberate role modelling and teaching;
5. allocation of rewards and status;
6. and recruitment, selection, promotion, and excommunication.

These reinforcing mechanisms only work if they are consistent with the primary mechanisms:

1. organisational design and structure;
2. organisational systems and procedures;
3. organisational rites and rituals;
4. design of physical environment;
5. stories, legends, and myths;
6. and statements of philosophy, values, and creed.

For example, best-in-class companies incorporate corporate values in the performance criteria *and* link bonus and promotion to the overall performance appraisal of employees. In performance ratings, the how objectives are reached and can be limited to the values for non-managers.

Some organisations align the salary process. For example, sixty percent of bonus is based on respect of values and twenty percent of performance-based rewards linked to how managers achieve results.

Some organisations align the promotion process. For example, lack of respect of values is a reason for being fired and is a criteria for assessment of promotability potential; as for external recruitment, values are go/no-go criteria for internal recruitments and mobility.

3.12.9. Repetition is key. What do you suggest to do ensure it ?

Yes, repletion is key. Role-modeling by the leaders is key in terms of embedding values. Another lever, is that values or behaviors that illustrate them are talked about regularly and with regards to concrete and daily activities.

The most symbolic and frequent activity workers engage in are meetings. Meetings are also an opportunity for concrete role-modeling by leaders.

So, something that has a strong impact in embedding values is to institutionalize the fact that every meeting ends with a five minutes discussion about "did we live and breath the values during the meeting?".

The goal is not to make a formal assessment and do reporting. Participants to the meeting select the one value or behavior to be discussed. The questions to ask are "did we live and breath this in the invitation process, the definition of the agenda, the reminder of context, the definition of the issues, the brainstorming of solutions, the decision-making, the closure, and so on. Each step of the meeting process is assessed against the value or the behavior. The discussion is ended with a commitment of things to do better for next meeting.

Putting a poster on the wall of each meeting room with these questions often helps to drive the discussion.

3.12.10 Who should be involved to define the values that sustain the change?

Ideally, it is the same people who defined the draft vision of the change. Once you have a draft of the new values, you validate them using online dialogue events.

An online dialogue event enables an organisation to involve people in the (re)definition of, for example, corporate values. It is a two- to three-day internet-based event during which people chat online, react to comments made by peers about a proposal of values, and rank their relevance. It sometimes ends up looking like an online brainstorming event. The analysis of the online activities enables the organisation to fine-tune the

Slim Lambert

proposal and weigh the importance of things for the people. You can extend the dialogue to address topics such as daily illustrations of a corporate culture such as "rituals," "heroes." and so on. *At this step of the process, you can afford to have a dialogue online* and not in face-to-face meetings because people have practiced true dialogue in previous steps, and, leaders have practiced reacting to and using empowerment in a constructive manner. Anybody and everybody can participate to the online dialogue event. People based all around the world can discuss in a synchronous manner. There are several collaborative tools that support these events (just to mention two of them, there is the IBM jams and feedback 2.0). Each person has maximum opportunity to elicit his or her ideas since the dialogue lasts for several days. The dialogue is often organized into a handful of separate forums, each on a different subtopic related to the overall topic.

3.13. DESCRIPTION OF THE WORKSHOP TO DEFINE THE DRAFT OF VALUES THAT SUPPORT THE CHANGE

This is the proposal of draft of values that will be used during the online dialogue event. It lasts for a couple of hours.

- **Step1. Agree on the organisational values to support the change.**

In subgroups, define three categories of values. For each of these categories, define those valued by employees and by stakeholders.

The three categories are:

- Core values. They are non-negotiable. They guarantee the change is not questioned. They are the organisation's current and historical values.
- Aspirational values. They are lacking today or they would reinforce the change.
- Permission-to-play values. They are symbolic or representative of what changing means at an individual level.

Define the values in the form of a scale. At the end of the scale are the proposed values. At the other end is its flip side— for example, from taking risks to playing it safe.

Then share the proposals in a plenary session. Go back into subgroups and combine all the different axis to define an even more reduced number of values. For example, add "control" to "risk taking" and it becomes "controlled risk taking."

In plenary sessions, locate the culture of the company somewhere along it, and define how many points you want to move on the axis. Then, agree on sentences that define each value. For example, "have a passion for excellence and hate bureaucracy; are open to ideas from anywhere and committed to work-out live quality and drive cost and speed for competitive advantage; have the self-confidence to involve everyone and behave in a boundary-less fashion to create a clear, simple, reality-based vision and communicate it to all constituencies; have enormous energy and the ability to energise others stretch by setting aggressive goals and rewarding progress; understand accountability and commitment; see change as opportunity, not a threat that has a global brain; build diverse and global teams."

Go back in subgroups, and for each value identified, add an anecdote illustrating the value in action. It can be real or imaginary. Anecdotes should explain how the value helps to solve a problem and avoid anxiety, while delivering a solution that embeds the change. During the online dialogue event, people could vote on the anecdotes that they think best illustrate each value.

- Step 2. Translate values into other elements: norms, rituals, and importance/ urgency criteria.

In subgroups, ask, how can we too live and breathe the value on a daily basis? Break into three groups.

One group brainstorms a list of ways visibly to signal each value to the rest of the organisation. These must be specific such as "meet with our distributors to get their ideas and feedback," not generalities like "communicate better."

Another group discusses ways that teams, and/or individuals on the team, often inadvertently violate each value.

These two groups are encouraged to think of measurable or visible elements such as:

- Key organisation systems, processes, and structures (Whom do they serve? Do they help or hinder people trying to live your values? For what are people rewarded and recognized?)
- Think of groups of customers, external partners, and internal people (What are the three things that our organisation or team seems to care about most?)
- Recent or current crisis (What values were really tested?)
- Dramatic, visible ways to demonstrate the new values.

The last group looks at ways teams and individuals can get feedback from others in the organisation on how well they are living the values.

3.14.1. Overview

The question that people ask is, How can our working environment enable us to meet today's business objectives in alignment with the defined change and to integrate the core requirements, maximising both productivity and an engaging work environment?

During the workgroup, people analyse their ways of working and redesign it. It is a method that enables people to participate directly in the redesign process. It uses dialogue to arrive at local solutions. *It locates responsibility for redesign activities and their implementation with those closest to the work.* It is a design process based on analyzing and fitting together the social system (people's skills, knowledge, experience, and relationship networks) and the technical system (the technical process by which the work gets done) to maximize both productivity, an engaging work environment, and the needs of the change.

First, participants analyse how their job is now done and then assess how far this falls short of meeting a set of criteria. They analyse their current work environment according to a set of criteria.

Second, they redesign for a better way of doing the work. They analyse their workflow and design their work unit according to the criteria that maximizes both productivity and an engaging work environment. These criteria are, for example, multi-skilling, responsibility for control and coordination within the workgroup itself, payment for skills (both social and technical), and joint responsibility for goal attainment.

Third, they work out how the new design could be implemented. They prescribe other actions needed to support their new work environment. The activities in this section include establishing measurable goals and objectives for the work group, identifying training requirements and immediate action steps, establishing career paths or skill blocks for developing the necessary skills, and explaining how their design will improve the scores on the six criteria used to initially analyse the work environment.

It provides employees with a process not only for improving their work environment but also for sustaining the change.

Examples of outcomes are:

- Team boundaries are negotiated within the overall vision and mission of the change.
- The roles of managers and supervisors are redesigned, and supports are defined to help them make the adjustments.
- The processes, tools, and workflows are reviewed or aligned.
- Job roles are changed in scope, which interfaces in the organisation or with expected outcomes.

In comparison to other popular redesign or reengineering methods, the Best Place to Work workshop aligns and redesigns work process and people's jobs. It is unique because of its benefits:

- People restructure their own workplace—they make their own choices and no designs are ever imposed.
- There is no transition period following redesign—implementation is immediate.
- The location of responsibility for coordinating and controlling new ways of working moves away from supervisors to the people who are actually doing the work.
- Actions to sustain the change for organisations, if needed, are driven by empowered and involved employees who are committed to these actions. The workshops produce high commitment in people to carry out their own designs.
- The outcome of the workshops is a highly flexible organisation that will have the ability to learn solutions continuously. Indeed, the redesign is done in line with principles that ensure adaptiveness of each person in their job. This is key to sustain the change. In addition, it builds the basis for an effective organisation that will need less change management programmes in the future. Adaptiveness, engagement, and little bureaucracy are also guiding principles of the redesign. The outcome is an organisation, structured around multi-skilled, self-managed groups with the capacity to learn without major external support.

- There is no need for a lengthy and expensive involvement of expert consultants or design teams, which can eat up organisational resources.

Indeed, one key shortcoming of classic existing redesign and restructuring processes is the reliance on "the internal expert/elite design group." There are a number of problems with this. First, even internal design teams are small and function as experts and cause as much resistance as any outside expert typically generates. Design teams normally learn an expert-driven method only at a superficial level. A small select or elite internal team with an agenda for changing everyone's job is not able to generate enough excitement and sense of ownership to drive adoption throughout an entire organisation. Such design teams often become pariahs to employees fearful of losing their jobs.

Second, "fixing" part of the system is unsystematic. Redesign initiatives that go in and tackle parts of the organisation to make them leaner and meaner, without working with the whole, create more havoc than success. Third, most classic work redesign strategies today impose expert solutions on the organisation and often take months just to gather data and conduct diagnostics. Of course, the people who already know all these data and diagnostics are the people that work there! Moreover, they already have ideas, and in many cases, strong views as to how their work units can be changed for the betterment of themselves, their peers, and the organisation as a whole. By pooling their initiatives for change, they can redesign their workplace themselves. Having people participate in the design of their own work establishes that every person, from the president to the frontline employee, can be a researcher, learner, teacher, and resource. It is a clear, conceptual understanding of the basic structure of work, change, and what motivates people to put their best foot forward that you need for this do-it-yourself work redesign method.

- The redesign process is fast. It takes no more than two days for people to redesign their own work unit.
- The way work is redesigned enhances motivation and commitment.

3.14.2. When you ask people to redesign their jobs and work environment, what set of criteria do they use?

A first set of criteria are those *specific to the change*. They can be the key behaviours defined in the vision of the change or the values that have been redefined in this last step of the REFRESHING change process.

The second set of criteria is what *motivates people to do excellent work, that is, the work condition criteria of a productive and engaging work environment*. The first three of these criteria relate to the content of a job. The second three requirements relate to the social climate of the workplace. All these requirements are criteria people would use to create a margin of manoeuvre to escape formal constraints that structure their environment. So what you do is to accept that there is this risk and live with it. You satisfy the need of people to create a margin of manoeuvre, and then start from that as a foundation for the alignment of processes. At least that way you know the alignment is a solution that will last, and one that represents what happens in the real world. These criteria are:

Autonomy and margin of manoeuvre. It is the feeling that you can influence your own work and that you don't have to ask permission for everything. It is having enough elbow room to feel empowered, but not so much that you do not know what to do. It is the feeling that you are your own bosses and that you are not being constantly scrutinized by a supervisor breathing down your neck.

Opportunity to learn continually on the job. It is the feeling that learning is possible because you can set goals that are reasonable challenges for you and get timely feedback on results, to make corrections, rather than being called on the carpet after the fact.

Optimum level of variety. It is the feeling that you can avoid boredom and fatigue and that you can vary your work, thus avoiding fatigue and boredom. It is the ability to set up your own satisfying rhythm of work through which you can be most productive.

Mutual support and respect. It is the feeling that you can and do get help and respect from your co-workers. Instead of being pitted against each other in a "someone has to win and someone has to lose" scenario, you can give and receive support and respect, enabling the group to cooperate and use all members' skills to the fullest.

Meaningfulness. It is the feeling that your own work meaningfully contributes to society or a higher purpose. It is also to have knowledge of the whole product or service to which you contribute. This sense of meaningfulness includes the quality of the product or service and its worth to the community.

A desirable future. Put simply, it is not having a dead-end job but one with a career path that will allow personal growth and increase in skills.

Empowered flexibility. It is the feeling that you can respond adequately to market demand because you can behave flexibly and adaptively. It is having the opportunity to broaden your roles outside of sheer job classifications. It is being able to develop skills in a wide variety of social and technical tasks to respond adequately and flexibly to demands placed on the work unit. You can perform multiple functions, tasks, and skills that can be applied when needed. You, therefore, have more value for the success of the whole organisation. Redundancy of skills occurs when you are skilled in a wide variety of social, business, and technical tasks and functions.

3.14.3. What is the cascading process of the Best Place to Work workshop?

The process of cascading is bottom-up, but inside a frame that is top-down. Solutions to redesign progress bottom-up, but decision-making criteria for these redesigns are imposed top-down. This way of cascading embeds a key principle used to solve dilemmas and define strategic decision: "manage one way and organise the other"?

In the first step, senior management define the minimum critical specifications against which all designs must be measured. An example of a minimum critical specification would be "no increase in staff" or "less than a 5 percent increase in budget" or "maintain the same level of customer service." In determining these specifications, management must be extremely careful to find a balance, providing enough specifications to give participants some guidance but without releasing an avalanche of rules that will smother the creative process.

Once lower levels are redesigned and functioning, the higher organisational levels are redesigned to support the previous level's redesign. After each work unit completes its redesign, the next phase in the process is to have their supervisors attend workshops and develop their own redesign. Each group, of course, should have full knowledge of the designs that came out of the first group's meetings. However, they are not required to follow that group's lead.

Often a series of parallel workshops is used to allow every person in similar work unit (similar in raison d'être or organisational level) to participate. Participants hold a "town meeting" in which the designs are discussed and integrated as much as possible. Finally, one design is selected by the workers.

What if the supervisor recommends a different design from what the employees propose? Let us say, for example, that work units at the same organisational level produce three designs: A, B, and C. Most of the workforce prefer design A, but the senior management preferred design C. A "fishbowl" meeting is organised to dialogue about the pros and cons of each option. (See below how to run a fishbowl meeting.)

How many people should be involved per workshop, and how long are the workshops? Best Place to Work cascading is a flexible process that can be adapted to fit organisational needs, its size, and its complexity. Each workshop usually consists of twenty to thirty-five people from a work unit working in small groups. If the work unit is small (four to twelve people), it is best if everybody works together on the design. When a larger section of the organisation is being redesigned, it is necessary to get wide participation that reflects a deep slice of the organisation. Mixed teams from the same work unit can work in parallel during the workshop and then integrate their designs. Or with larger units, teams can participate in separate workshops and integrate their designs later during town hall meetings. If there are significant disagreements about the design, run a fishbowl meeting. Otherwise, run a simple sharing of perspectives meeting.

Are stakeholders involved? No. There is a pre-work to integrate stakeholder input. Stakeholders are not physically present. Instead, data are collected from stakeholders ahead of time. In some instances, stakeholders can be brought in to give input and to answer questions. They are not, however, part of creating, redesign, or the meeting. This is based on the belief that the people building the design should be the ones who are, in the end, responsible for implementation, because they are the ones who have to live with it and make it work. However, stakeholders should be invited as management discusses the proposals made by their lower levels as an output of the previous Best Place to Work workshops.

3.14.4. A facilitator's guide and a description of the steps of the best place to work

Step 1: Assessment of our immediate job environment.

- The workshop begins with general introductions and a run through of the agenda, explaining the purpose and process of each part.
- Then there is the presentation of the criteria for the redesign defined by senior management.
- Participants have a discussion about characteristics of an organisation that do not apply to these criteria. The focus is on the shortcomings of such an organisation.
- The participants working the criteria and skills matrices. Participants work in groups to analyse their jobs as they exist. They do this by completing two matrices.

First, they analyse their jobs by tabulating, comparing, and discussing their scores on the set of criteria, using a scale from -5 to +5. Valuable but previously hidden data about the nature of their workplace and their social infrastructure is revealed.

Second, they analyse the skills they possess. Participants compare the current skills with the needed skills. This analysis helps them create a gap analysis, which is then used to plan training and staff development opportunities (what training, for how long, whether it should occur on or off the job and to what levels).

- Reporting.

Groups report their findings from the matrix analysis. The pattern of scores is used as a diagnostic tool immediately. The findings will also be taken into account later, during the redesign phase. When participants identify suggestions for changing boundaries and changes that are outside their workgroups, these suggestions are outside the boundary of step 1. They are recorded to be considered during step 2.

Step 2: Redesign of our work environment (structure and workflows)

Participants identify and analyse how they need to transform their work processes. As they discuss this, they also make plans to assure that their new work processes conform to the guidelines defined by the senior management.

Participants are now ready to focus on redesigning their structure.

- Working on current structure and workflow.

Work unit participants draw the existing workflow and organisational structure so that everyone knows where decisions are currently made. First, groups lay out their current process or workflow on a chart.

Then they draw up the current organisational structure, as it is real jobs, real people. Then they go to that structure and start sorting out a redesign consistent with the guiding criteria.

The new organisational chart will have to be absolutely clear about the boundaries around their groups—what is in and what is out.

- Work unit participants redesign for a better, more natural way of doing the work, incorporating the criteria.

First, they describe desirable characteristics for the organisational design of the work unit and support work units. Then they invent more effective ways to relate to the external environment.

The new designs will be measured against the fact that they support the guiding criteria defined by senior management.

During a plenary session, groups present and compare their initial design options. Other groups give feedback and suggestions for improvements, implementation practicalities, and issues that must be taken into account in final designs.

- Then the various design teams create action plans to implement the proposed new designs.

Management returns to the workshops to listen, discuss, and negotiate with the group. Teams must develop their own full range of goals, addressing operational, business, human resources, and technical areas. Initial team goals will still require negotiation with middle management to ensure targets are consistent with and support the overall organisational vision and goals.

At this point, teams specify additional organisational arrangements that will be required to become supportive of the guiding criteria defined by senior management. These might include feedback mechanisms, equipment, job rotation procedures, support needed from other groups, and staffing needs.

3.14.5. A meeting tool to support the Best Place to Work workshop: fishbowl meeting.

Overview.
The objective of the fishbowl meeting tool is to find common ground on a controversial issue and to learn giving and receiving feedback. This technique can be used in problem solving because it helps participants gather insight about other participants' points of view and opinions. It can also be used to create understanding of the ladder of inference for two opposing groups of participants. The value of the fishbowl workshop

is that it creates a space that enables participants to observe, discover, and analyse other participants' thought processes.

A fishbowl workshop uses a format in which some participants form a discussion circle, while the remaining participants form a listening circle around the discussion group. Each group has an opportunity to discuss the issue of the meeting while the other group observes, rather like looking at fish in a fish bowl. The goal is for one group to experience the others' discussion without debating or challenging it. This ensures that the other group of participants has enough discussion time.

What happens during a fishbowl meeting?
A maximum of four subgroups are organized, based on their different points of view on the theme of the meeting. Several people representing point of view A talk together, while those representing point of view B sit in the audience. After a set period of time (maximum fifteen minutes), the A participants move into the audience and are replaced in the fishbowl by the B participants, who talk among themselves while the A participants watch and listen. If there are more than two point of view groups, this is done for the other groups, in order for all participants to listen to all points of view. Then a summary and debrief are organized by the facilitator.

Why is fishbowl more productive than a debate?
Because people are talking with their fellow partisans, they get less caught up in pointless confrontational games. Each participant is encouraged to spend their brief time providing others with evidence and logic to support their main points

Slim Lambert

in the light of what others have said. The small group conversations in the fishbowl tend to depersonalise the issue and reduce the stress level, making people's statements more constructive. Furthermore, real dialogue among same-side partisans often reveals significant differences among them—or other facets and nuances of the issue usually hidden if there was a debate instead of a dialogue. In a debate, the point is for one side to win. In a dialogue, like fishbowl, the point is to clarify issues and evidence and perhaps along the way to discover new perspectives, understandings, and options that may not have occurred to anyone earlier. When dialogue in any form goes well, people's positions tend to soften or break down, to be replaced by greater understanding.

A facilitator's guide and a description of steps of a fishbowl

Arrange chairs in a fishbowl configuration (two concentric circles). Radiating out from that, you have more rows of chairs. You could have a few more rows if you have a large group. Those in the centre can either be selected or volunteer from the group. This is a choice you need to make based on your goals. For example, if you know there are several people with different opinions, you can make sure those vocal people are in there at the beginning. Letting those who have passion about a topic or issue step forward is also a good way too.

Ask those from point of view A group to sit in the discussion circle, and ask point of view B group (and point of view C group, if applicable) to take their places in the outer-circle seats. Remember, chairs are positioned into two circles—an inner circle facing each other and an outer circle surrounding the inner circle. Members of the outer circle are able to view the discussion but are asked not to discuss anything among themselves.

Critical to the success of fishbowl activities is that the observing participants do not share their reflections right away, but give the participants in the fishbowl an opportunity to demonstrate what they know. Ask your first question for discussion and allow up to fifteen minutes for discussion. As the facilitator, you can direct the opening of the conversation and then let go.

A variation on this would be to break the conversation that the centre is having and go around the audience (the outer circles) to see what people are thinking about the centre conversation. This creates a feedback loop and lets the rest of the room express itself.

The role of the facilitator is to be a moderator. Moderating should be kept at a minimum, except for keeping the conversation wandering too far off track. The facilitator is responsible for encouraging discussion during the small group discussion, keeping the discussion only among the inner circle, and then drawing out individual and group reactions during the combined discussion later. If you wish, ask one of the participants to lead the discussion. The facilitator focuses the discussion on facts rather than assumptions. The combined group discussion should focus on bringing out discoveries about the other group. Participants often note that it is more difficult to be outside the fishbowl observing than it is being a member of the group being observed. They may even express frustration with the process and have difficulty understanding what is gained by observation. So the facilitator may have to manage these frustrations and questions at the appropriate time.

Next, invite the members of point of view B group to sit in the inner circle, replacing "point of view A" group members, who now move to the outer circle. Ask the members of group 2 if they would like to make any brief comments about the first discussion, and then plunge into the discussion. If you have decided to split the participants into more than two groups, continue with group 3.

Reconvene the group and ask participants for their overall thoughts about the topic discussed. When time runs out, the fishbowl is closed and the facilitator summarizes the discussion. Invite each subsequent group to respond to the discussion of the other group(s).

5. CONCLUSION: IF A CHANGE MANAGER IS THE ONE WHO HELPS A LEADER OF AN ORGANISATION DELIVER A CHANGE, WHAT SHOULD HIS OR HER ROLE BE, AND WHERE IN THE COMPANY ORGANISATION SHOULD HE OR SHE BE?

SHOULD THE CHANGE MANAGER BE LOCATED INSIDE THE CORPORATE UNIVERSITY?

Yes, if the corporate university:

- is more than just reinforcing and perpetuating a winning formula;
- and is the vehicle for the adjustment of the organisation's practices, systems, policies, strategies or even underlying values and helps "learners" explore the ambiguous, the uncomfortable, and the unknown.

Corporate university, more than any other forum in the organisation, offers the ideal neutral environment for each of the above. It is a "safe house" or laboratory for questioning, wondering, exploring, and, perhaps most importantly, challenging with a critical mass of externally and internally-focused people, while receiving process support.

This is one of the ways to set up major changes with the right expertise and resources to succeed. As mentioned, it could be part of the corporate university or of a department in the corporate centre, for example in the HR, innovation, or culture function.

This department will set up changes for success in an integrated fashion, for the good of the overall enterprise. It will create synergies of resources and talents. It is the most efficient when it is the centre of a network of full-time or part-time change ambassadors accountable for implementing change for different parts of the organisation.

There is an economy of scale consideration: a change manager can serve several internal clients, and not all change efforts require a full-time resource. Actually, it is highly recommended to promote to part-time change manager an employee who could use this experience as a stepping stone for their career progression. In the network model, the department has access to a myriad of expertise and resources that may be needed for any change to succeed and has the authority to mobilize and organize the right resources for a given change effort.

The department does not "own" all of these resources. Rather, it recognizes the full menu of resources in the organisation that can be tapped to play a role in change—just in time and well aligned with the change strategy. And where it recognizes a critical gap in in-house competency, it can sponsor the development or hiring of that set of services so that the organisation's changes have a greater likelihood to succeed.

Many profiled groups have actively built up a pool of external consultants whom they regularly employ or to whom they direct others in the company. But beware. The department can't do it alone. Managing change is the responsibility of the leader of the organisation. The department's role is to put in place the resources, processes, tools, and methods to coach if needed by the leader to drive the change effectively. To do this, the department works in tandem with change ambassadors. The department helps ambassadors establish a plan for the change management process and animates the REFRESHING meeting tools. The department acts as a mentor, focused on actions and on developing change ambassadors' learning and accountability.

The mission of the change management department is to increase the organisation's capability to adapt and adopt new ways of doing business. And the role of the department is the same as the one of change ambassadors when the change theme proposed by the leader is transversal to begin.

Thanks to its central positioning, the role of the department is to help ensure a global synergy and prioritization of change initiatives based on alignment with the global organisation's strategic objectives. It ensures overall consistency of change processes at both a strategic and an operational level. The role

Slim Lambert

of the department is also to handling the power issues for the leader who solicits support from change ambassadors.

Should the department or its ambassadors report directly to the leader of the change?

Very often leaders of an organisation must, in the context of a change, receive advice and some tough feedback—especially if they have been used to classic change management approaches. And this cannot truly be done if the leader is your boss.

A key success factor is that the leader does role modelling. Telling the leader of his or her own shortcomings and areas for improvement can be tricky. It can't be done if the leader is the boss of the ones who says this. A strong, independent board, a healthy governance system, and a strong performance evaluation process can help. But these mechanisms are not a substitute for the ongoing feedback that leaders need from the change management department or ambassadors.

Change managers need to be independent. Few dare, and rightfully so, to confront the leader on critical issues they report directly to the leader. The change manager ensures the leader is prepared to ask themselves two of the most difficult questions of all: To what extent am I part of the problem? and, harder yet, To what extent am I part of the solution? Only when they address these difficult questions honestly and openly can leaders begin the vital task of changing their own mindset and behaviour in order to be a role model. It cannot be done if the leader is the boss of the change manager.

Change managers should be close to the leader, without reporting directly to him or her. The change manager needs the freedom and authority to get the leader's attention and enable rapid course corrections when a major change needs it. This can only be done as a colleague, or perhaps a boss, but not as a subordinate.

Today's organisations can no longer look at managing change as a "black box." It is time to see change management as a critical organisational discipline that will be required for a successful tomorrow. Having a change management department and a network of ambassadors is a good start.

Good luck.

www.ingramcontent.com/pod-product-compliance
Lightning Source LLC
Chambersburg PA
CBHW071402170526
45165CB00001B/155